Paperback ISBN: 979-8-218-33127-6
Hardcover ISBN: 979-8-218-34046-9
eBook ISBN: 979-8-218-33128-3
Library of Congress Control Number: 2024900009

Cover and book design by Jason Arias

Printed in the United States of America

Becoming Home

Journeying Through the Rooms
of My Past to Reclaim My Story

Ashleigh Stevens

Dedication

To my four siblings that came before me, you mean the entire world to me.

To my parents, for your constant love and support.

To my daughters, for simply being yourselves. I'm so lucky to be your mom.

To my husband, for believing in me and pushing me to pursue my dreams.

To Coach A., for seeing the woman I could one day become.

To Tycee, for saving my life. None of this would be possible without you.

Author's Note

"*Vulnerability is not weakness, and the uncertainty, risk,*

and emotional exposure we face every day are not optional.

Our only choice is a question of engagement."

–Brené Brown, *Daring Greatly*

Due to the sensitive nature of this memoir, some names and details have been changed. Some people were combined with others to make one character, and some dates, timelines, and locations were altered, all to protect privacy. This is my story, and all the events in this memoir are as true as I can remember.

While I am proud of my story and the struggles I went through, it is not my right to tell anyone else's story, but my own. I am perfectly comfortable showing the world myself and my truths, but I want to respect that others may not feel the same. It is not my goal to expose or get revenge. It is my goal to share, connect, and bring hope to others like me. It is my goal to tell my story, without hurting anyone else in the process. It is my goal, to help others find healing while joining me on this journey through my rooms.

Entryway

Home has never been one place for me.

I lived in so many different homes growing up. I had the one I grew up in, the one we were in until I was ten. I had the two in Texas, the year we lived there. I had my stepfather's house and the three rentals we lived in each time my mom and I left him. I had the one on Bear Dance. The few with my dad. The one with Kendra. The list goes on.

Home has never been a place to me because the place is always changing. Home is a person, it is people. Home is my family, my siblings. I'm the last of five siblings: Ryan, Keena, Kendra, Scott, and me. My mom is at the heart of the five of us, she is the one who brought us together. We all share the same mom, but Scott and I are the only ones who share our dad. My sister Keena always says, "It's a confusing family tree, it's more like a tumbleweed, but it is a beautiful one." She's right, and I wouldn't trade it for anything normal.

I have always felt a sense of home when thinking about my siblings. I love being a part of a big family, I love the closeness I feel to them. I love that at any moment I have multiple places I could go to and various people I could call to feel safe and supported.

Over the last few years, I've come to experience home in myself. For so long there were rooms in my memories that I had closed off and barred. There were so many places that I never wanted to revisit. Trauma that I wanted to ignore. But in closing off those rooms, I kept myself from experiencing true healing, knowing myself and loving myself as I was, and entering new rooms that would bring life and joy.

After I finally ended a toxic relationship, I decided it was time to investigate those rooms. But I didn't want to do it alone. I would have to let someone in with me. Into the mess, pain, fear, and heartbreak. And I figured it might as well be a complete stranger.

It was my first time going to therapy, and I was terrified. I almost left before my first therapy session started—feeling so overwhelmed by it. Just as I considered leaving, letting my fear get the best of me, a blonde woman opened the door, "Ashleigh?" she asked. As I take in my therapist, her presence is warm and inviting. She has kind eyes and a perfectly styled haircut that sits just below her chin with beach waves styled throughout it. Somehow, without ever knowing this woman, I immediately felt extremely safe. I step into her room and find my place on her couch. It is much cozier here than I expected. It doesn't feel like a doctor's office at all, it feels like a home.

After a few visits, one of my first tasks was to make a timeline of my life. I was to write down all those big memories that come to mind when I look back on my life. What seemed like simple homework, quickly became a daunting task. My life was full of so many beautiful moments, but in this homework, those weren't the memories that came to me. It was the tough ones, the ones that demanded change from me that came pouring back.

Perhaps it's because the tough times shape you more than the good ones. The good ones are easy, you simply get to enjoy them. I started as far back as I could remember, the very first memory of my life: my mom and dad fighting. The memory ended up being the last major fight my parents had right before they got divorced. I don't have many details, I just remember the fight, the fear that I felt, and the changes that came right after.

I continued on my timeline, documenting my brother's diagnosis and the death that changed our family forever, and I ended with the traumatic breakup I had just endured. Granted, I was eighteen years old when I did this, so that was where the memories had stopped. The timeline quickly was soaked in a mess of tears that began to fall uncontrollably from my face. I let every tear fall willingly until I was a limp and saturated mess. This was perhaps the first time I had ever shown true empathy for myself and it felt so heavy.

I stared at that timeline, and I felt so incredibly sad for me. It broke my heart that I had this beautiful life clouded by these big and immensely painful events. So many of which, I assumed were somehow my own fault. I wanted to save that girl from her past. I wanted the pain to stop, just for one moment, to pretend that none of it had ever happened. But the pain wouldn't stop, the memories wouldn't fade, and the past could not be rewritten. So, I did what I could and I grieved.

I cried for all of those moments that I shoved down before. I cried for the many versions of myself that felt alone, bottled up, and masked away. I cried and I cried, until I made my way back to myself, to my true self, not to the buttoned-up version the world told me I should be. Not to the version my ex wanted me to be. But to the real me. To the girl, who like everyone else, has things in her life that really hurt. The girl, like so many others, lost herself because of it.

This was my first step on the road to becoming who I am today because once we had the timeline done, we knew exactly where to start. These main life events gave us a series of rooms that needed to be opened, cleaned up, and most importantly understood. See, some of these rooms had been haunting me for years, so the last thing I wanted to do was step inside. I knew exactly what rooms the monsters were in, why would I willingly enter those rooms? It gave me comfort knowing that I would not be going in alone, but that terrified me even more because someone was officially going to see me for all that I was.

I had this horrible idea that these rooms in my mind were the things that made me less than others. I remember even describing them as stains and dents, things that made me undeserving and unworthy of love. It never made sense to me that I could love so many people with flaws just like mine, but when it came to looking at myself, anything less than perfect simply was not enough. These impossible standards set me up for self-deprecating language that played through my mind like a broken record. Many phrases that I heard from others became a mantra in my own head.

"You aren't good enough."

"It's all your fault."

"You could have fought back."

I had to find a way to change the narrative because these voices were killing me from the inside out.

The only way out of the darkness is through it. I had to go back through my timeline. I needed to go see what everything truly was, but from the perspective of an adult and not a child. I needed to go into every room, I needed to see the entire ugly mess that each one was, and then I could share how I cleaned it up and made it out.

Perhaps we all have these rooms, some of our rooms may even look vaguely similar. If in any way, anyone can connect to my experiences or emotions, hopefully, I can help others feel a little less alone and a little more loved. Hopefully, I can share my story and help people like me.

I am not an expert. I am just a woman who struggled like most people to become the person that I am today. The person, I believe, I was meant to be. So, hopefully, with my honesty, I can help others feel less alone or inspire them to be true to themselves and honor what they've been through. All of us have these reels, those amazing and traumatizing images in our heads. The issues we struggle to outgrow. The hard part isn't admitting that they exist, you know that they do, and you have known that for years. The hard part is living a fulfilling life anyway. To accept them, to dive into them, to connect with others because of them. To use them to become a better person, create a better life and maybe one day, help those around you.

Writing this is terrifying, telling the world who you are and everything you went through is scary. It's vulnerable and on one hand, it can set you up for judgment, but on the other, it can set you up for so much more. What greater gift can I offer myself, my daughters, or other women like me? I needed to learn how to own my story, and how to care about me. This is me doing that. These are my rooms.

Chapter 1: Unhinged

My therapist pulls out my timeline, stares at the blue paper and she starts poking around the events to see what room we should go in first. To me, the answer is easy. I need to go into the room I just left. I need to unpack everything that happened in my relationship that I just ended. I need to understand how I got here in the first place. I need to learn how to make sure I never get here again.

It only made sense to start with the most recent event and work our way down the timeline. It would not go in chronological order, it seems the brain doesn't really store things that way. This will be the first metaphorical door I see. It will be the first time that I allow myself to indulge in the past in hopes to find answers. When I see the door, it looks exactly as it should. Cream in color and ripped off the hinges. A close eye can see that something went wrong here, that this door has seen some things. As much as I don't want to, I reach for the handle. I know the only way out is through. I take a timid step inside and close my eyes. There. She. Is.

The first thing I see is myself on the floor. I am crying and I can just barely make out the words if I listen carefully enough, "I will get therapy. I don't know what's wrong with me. I can change. I have to change. I know it's all my fault. Please stay with me," I am pleading.

I remember the fight well because it only happened a few weeks ago. Who knew that a "Happy Birthday" text would be the last straw? That it would be enough for my boyfriend, Cody, to completely lose it. To erupt. To send him into such a rage that I would lock myself in our bathroom and try to hide and wait out his storm. I sat as far as I could away from that door as I heard him jerk on the handle and bang on the wood.

As I sit here, I pray to God that He won't let the door open. I hold my legs in my arms as I sit on the cold tile floor and mentally I begin to beg my brain to take me anywhere else. *God, please take me somewhere else.* A tried and true survival strategy that I practiced as a kid. I close my eyes and He takes me.

Those door hinges would later need replacing as he broke them off trying to get to me. I so often went back to that version of myself, the one behind the locked door, sobbing for safety. I was here as a kid and now I am here again as an adult. The only real difference now was, I put myself here. I drove myself to this place, I chose to put up with this, for reasons I never understood. This one was on me.

By the time he got the door opened, he jerked me up ready for a fight. I blocked so much of it out, it's hard to remember any of the words we said. There was so much noise and before I knew what was happening, I flew back into the wall and my head slammed against the frame hanging up behind me. The glass shattered to the floor and so did the girl who hit it.

I saw two things when he shoved me, the first was the angry, dark eyes of my stepfather. The second, was my future if I didn't get out, if I didn't get the help I needed.

I got up onto my knees and laid my head down in prayer, glass all around me, "I will go to therapy. I don't know what's wrong with me. I can change. I have to change. I know it's all my fault. Please stay with me" I begged both of God and myself.

* * *

My friend texted me "Happy Birthday" and as small as it seems, it really upset my boyfriend, Cody. The friend is a guy and even though I have never cheated on Cody, he has a list of reasons why this isn't an okay thing to do. Of why he doesn't trust me.

"You earned this," he reminded me.

I guess I did. He didn't trust me because I hid things, it was a strategy I used for protection. I would hide where I was, who I was with, and what I was doing because I knew that if he found out that I was at a party with my friends, he would lose his temper. Only he was allowed to do those things. I was not.

So, I hid things that were not worth the fight. We have been together since I was sixteen, and being with my friends doesn't seem like something I can give up, but I can keep a secret or two. I want freedom with my friends, and I don't know how to have it both ways.

The harder he tries to control me, the more I lash out. I am unwilling to give up anything, so I lie and hide, hoping that this way, I don't have to.

This is my first real relationship and I just assume that this jealousy and control is a token of love. He loves me so much. That's why he is like this. That's why he worries all the time. That's why he has me dye my hair, change my clothes, get rid of my high heels. I am "too tall for them anyways" as he says. In some ways, I guess he is right because even though I love myself the way I am, I am willing to give up all the things I love about myself to make him happy.

He knows better than I do. The blonde in my hair is okay too, it isn't the dark hair I prefer, but he likes this better. He always asks me to get more of it. So, I do. I get blonder, I dress how he likes, I throw away my heels, and I become the version of myself that can be worthy of his love. I become as small as possible. Which is hard to do at 5'8." But I am trying. That's how he likes me. So small, that the real me isn't even here anymore.

And after this fight on my eighteenth birthday, I know I've lost more of myself in this relationship than I realized. It makes me even madder at myself for not leaving him sooner, for not following through, for not fighting harder.

* * *

I think back to a memory from earlier on in our relationship. I see us on the dirty couch immediately. This experience foreshadowed just how much I would struggle to find my voice in this relationship and just how much it would mirror my childhood.

My boyfriend thinks it will be cute. I can tell by the way he is smiling when he reaches over and tries to start a playful wrestling match with me. Most girls would erupt in laughter, maybe it could even turn romantic like some ridiculously cute rom-com movie. But for me, it brings up a whole lot more. I do not think it is cute. The pit in my stomach is growing and before I start to fight him off, the tears start falling from my eyes. At first, he thinks it's funny. Like I am fighting back because I am so ticklish, and I just can't take it. But then, he sees it. My face is full of tears. His expression immediately turns from playful to confused.

"Stop," I say pushing my head away from his, trying to hide my face and my feelings.

He reaches for my chin and turns my head to his. His light eyes don't fill with empathy, instead, they look at me in discontent. They look at me and I can feel the disappointment.

"Seriously, please stop," I say as I get up to get away from him, ruining the moment.

This isn't flirtatious to me, it's terrifying. And before I can even become aware of why I am reacting this way to something so innocent, my face is soaking wet from crying. He probably thinks I am a total freak. I make up a dumb excuse to go home and the second my butt hits that leather seat in my car, the one my dad got me for my sixteenth birthday, the tears are flooding.

What was that? I can't bring myself to drive away just yet, even though I am dying to. I literally can't move. I throw my head back a few times. I take my frustration out on these seats. I am begging my body to just tell me what the heck is wrong with me. I stop to breathe, wrap my arms around myself and close my eyes in an attempt to calm myself down. That's when I see him. I keep seeing his face when my eyes are closed.

I force myself to keep them shut. To let myself go back to that memory, to try and dig out a reason for what I am feeling now. Even though it's been six years, I can still feel his hands on my wrists, the pain feels so close even though it was long ago. I beg him to stop, and my tiny frame squirms under his grip. He thinks this is hilarious.

I cry for him to "please just let me go."

He doesn't, not yet. I squeeze my eyes shut even tighter. He holds me down, hovering over me, and as he does, he lets spit drool out of his mouth. He doesn't let it fall though, he just taunts me with the disgusting threat of spitting on his stepdaughter.

I don't know what he gets out of this. I don't know how holding down a twelve-year-old girl is fun. I don't know why he would want to scare me. I don't know why he would want to humiliate me. It is a disgusting feeling and it makes me feel worthless. Like I am beneath, like I am someone who deserved to be spit on. Even though I was only twelve, I was old enough that I could tell it was bringing him an uncomfortable amount of pleasure.

The worst part about closing my eyes is that I have to see his eyes when I do. While he does this to me. His eyes are big and bulging. There is no warmth there, all I can see is a dark emptiness like no one lives inside. I try not to look into them. I avoid it at all costs. I look at the cream-colored carpet next to me, I pretend this isn't me that he's doing this to.

This is one of his favorite "games." He's just messing around, it's funny. That's what he'll say when I tell my mom. But I don't think it's funny, no one does. I hate him and I hate this.

It makes me feel small, disgusting, and weak. But when I cry about it, he laughs more. I am overreacting, I am sensitive. I am always overreacting and I am always sensitive. Of course, it's a game, this is my fault. *Why am I so weird? Why am I so sad over a game?*

This is my internal war. I open my eyes. Now, I knew why I hated wrestling so much. *He took that from me.* I start to drive home, my deepest thoughts always come to me when I am driving. It's the one place where I feel safe enough to let the feelings come to me. I let the hard memories flood back, and as they do they paint a picture of problematic patterns. I haven't thought of many of these moments since my mom and I left my stepdad, but now, in my current relationship, they keep coming up more frequently. I keep getting triggered and I don't understand why.

My boyfriend can shove me to the ground, and I will convince myself that I am the crazy one. That it is somehow my fault, and I am overreacting. *He is just joking, right? Or maybe it is my fault? I don't know.* All I know is that, in this car right now it is becoming clearer that I don't trust myself at all when it comes to judgment. I can't seem to separate myself now from twelve-year-old me. I can't seem to fully recognize the patterns that are right in front of me. The habits that would lead me into the darkest corners of my mind.

What a toxic recipe. What an easy target he made me.

As soon as I get home, I go to my room. Just before I go to bed, I send a text to Cody.

"I'm sorry. I don't know what's wrong with me."

But I did know, deep down. I just didn't want to accept it, didn't want to remember.

My boyfriend forgave me, for "overreacting" to the tickling incident, but I am still struggling to move on. I need answers. I need to know why my memories are coming back to haunt me. Months passed after I had this first breakthrough. While it feels like traveling back in time in the worst of ways, I am beginning to learn how crucial it is to remember. I just can't figure out how to make sense of my memories and I can't figure out why they are affecting me worse now than they were when it was actually happening.

* * *

As the tickling memory fades from my mind, another memory replaces it. It all started with my phone buzzing on the dark wooden nightstand in the middle of the night. It always starts with my phone buzzing. The vibration is just loud enough to wake me. It was late, so I felt like I better check it just in case it was an emergency. I reach over to grab my phone so I can read the text, it takes my eyes a second to wake up enough to see the blue bubble light up on my screen "You could do so much better than him."

This isn't the first time my best friend has said this to me. I knew something like this would set my boyfriend off, so I attempted to delete it. These were the kind of things I hid from him, I figured it was better this way. As I move my thumb over my screen to delete the message, he wakes up.

"What is that?" he says quickly as he sits up in bed.

I must have made a face. My face always gives me away before my mouth does. He immediately reaches to swat my phone out of my hands, but I manage to jump out of bed fast enough to avoid it. I get to the door instantly, it's only two steps away from his bed. The room is tiny, and I am out of it before a second passes.

As soon as I am out, I shut the door behind me and run down the stairs. I know I have to move fast. I have to give myself time to get rid of it. I almost fell down the stairs as I struggled to navigate my phone and the handrail as I sprinted down each step. Luckily, the stairs are carpet and I know them well. It's a straight shot down and within less than a minute I am down those stairs and have the text deleted.

As I hear him on the stairs, fear sets in.

I am not naive to his reactions. I know that the fact that I deleted the message, will only make him crazier to read it. I just don't know what that looks like.

I pass the living room and make my way to the kitchen. It's enclosed and small. The off-white colors are old and dated, and as I look around I see the dark wooden table in front of me. I decided my best bet was to stand behind it. I hope it will create a barrier between us. But, when he hits that last step and turns to me, I know that I'm screwed.

I run. I am running around the table, watching him closely to see when to change my direction. To keep the table between us.

I wasn't expecting this, but I am not surprised. I am unwilling to find out what happens when he catches me. I feel like I am going to throw up. I clutch the table and stop to breathe, it's the only thing keeping me up. I feel small. I feel stupid. I stare at him across the table and wonder why I put up with this type of behavior. *Why have I done it for years?*

I throw my phone on the table, and I run to my left, knocking down the chairs as I go. I hope it will slow him down, but he doesn't chase after me. He has what he wants. He can have my phone, but I won't let him have me. I run upstairs and step into his room, lock the door, and sink to the ground.

I cry into my hands with my back pushed against the door.

What is wrong with you? I ask myself.

Why are you still here?

The voice in my head is growing louder.

You are so stupid to stay here. It screams at me.

I am young and I am afraid. But all I see is a dumb girl begging to be loved.

Why is it always like this?

He plugs my phone into his desktop and tries everything he can to break into it. He stays downstairs, trying to hack into it for hours. It doesn't work. I get lucky. Eventually, with my head hanging low and my self-worth even lower, I drag myself up to unlock his bedroom door. I crawl into his bed and I cry my sorry self to sleep. I know I need to change. I know I can't stay here.

The longer I stay, the more lost I become. When I am with him and when I am in this room looking back, I see just how much I lost myself to him, to this relationship. It took so much more of me than I wanted to admit. This is not the type of nostalgia I enjoy. I'm ready to get what I need out of this room and never look back.

Chapter 2: When Your No is Ignored

It will be my eighteenth birthday tomorrow and as I celebrate becoming an adult, I want to feel like I actually have myself together, even though I know I don't. I want to wake up tomorrow and get a fresh start. I want to figure out a way to leave the past behind me. All I know is that I don't trust my judgment anymore. This room in my head is the hardest for me to understand. It's hard to imagine myself here at all. I never belonged here. But for now, I have to stay. I have more to clean up.

"Hello," I answer the phone in my groggy voice.

"Are you sleeping?" the hyper voice of my sister spits out.

"Yeah. I mean it is six in the morning, Keena."

"I know! I want to be the first one to wish you a happy birthday Ash-ba-dash-a-lot!"

"You always are" my voice cracks out with a smile.

"Go back to sleep Dash, I love you."

"I love you, Kee. Thank you."

I can't go back to sleep, but I wake up every birthday this way. To a phone call from my big sister. Her undeniable love and competitive nature motivate her to prove herself as the one who loves me the most every year. Even though she lives a whole state away from me, she makes Texas feel a lot less far from Colorado with her daily calls and reminders that she is always with me, even when she's not.

I wish she was with me now because my birthday, which I have been anticipating for years, is quickly turning from the best day to what feels like the worst. Later that day, I'd receive the birthday message that would send Cody into a fit of rage. His shoving me against the wall broke the spell, and I finally knew I needed to leave.

Later that night, I had dinner with my dad. And he looked at me with sad eyes and said, "Ashleigh, I just don't know about him. I don't think he's good for you."

He doesn't know how right he is. He doesn't know about the incident that happened just a few hours ago, and I had no intention of telling him.

He has been saying this to me for years, since the day I brought Cody home.

My entire family has, along with all of my friends. They see everything that I refuse to tell them. But as the years continued to pass, they gave up on me leaving him and I did too. And no one was saying anything anymore.

"Eventually, you will see how bad this really is and you'll leave him. I just hope it comes sooner than later" my father continues.

It's like he can read my mind. It's like he knows what I have planned.

"Dad, I know" I respond. I keep my eyes on the table, if there is disappointment in his eyes, I don't want to see it.

I am so stuck in my head. I know I am leaving Cody tomorrow. I know it is the right thing, I know I must, and I want to. But I am scared to be alone. My dad is hardly ever here, he is a state away taking care of my brother, Scott. All my siblings have moved on with their lives. I am alone and I am drowning, but I feel like no one can see me. I am dying for them to see me. To save me. I felt selfish for needing saving, but damn I was praying for it.

I knew that if I asked for help, either one of my parents would jump in for me, along with any one of my siblings. I just didn't even know how to admit that I needed it. That I needed them. They were all going through so much that I felt like I was not allowed to add to that burden. I needed to figure it out for myself, but I was swinging blind.

After a long pause, my dad let out a sigh. I knew my dad did not want to leave me here, I could see it in his eyes. As he poked at his food he said, "Please just come to Texas with me. You can be there with me and Scott, take some time off school."

He knew I was going to hit rock bottom here. He could see it. He assumed if he could get me away from Cody, he would help me avoid it. What he could not have known was how badly I needed to hit it.

"I can't go, Dad, I have to stay in school" I replied.

I could see how much it hurt my dad. He knew both of his kids were struggling, but he just couldn't save us both at the same time. No one could. I know that he knew in his heart that I needed him, and he tried to do everything he could to be there. But people can only help as much as you allow them, and as much as I begged for saving, I wasn't ready for it yet.

I needed to crash and burn, I needed to hit the lowest point. That was the only way I was going to be able to reinvent myself. To become someone, even I could love. My father kissed my cheek and wrapped his strong arms around me. I was sure this was the biggest hug he had ever given me.

"I will come back home soon honey, I love you," he said, "hang in there."

* * *

What was wrong with me? How could I get to this place? This place where my dad was so worried about me. In the beginning, before I was in too deep, it was just fun. I never planned on dating Cody seriously. I was not attracted to him, I did not want a boyfriend, I was just looking for a distraction from my pain and he gave it to me.

I was young and naive, desperate for love. But this is not what love is. This is a re-run of my past. While I was a perfectionist, in some parts of myself, I was dying to chase the wrong thing. I was dying to mess up, make mistakes, and be carefree, and he was the epitome of everything that I was not.

After we started dating, I tried to stay as close to my moral compass as possible, which meant saying "no" all the time. But he did not take "no" for an answer in the beginning and he would not start now. Slowly, but surely my voice became something only my mind would hear.

"I don't want to do this. I'm not ready."

"Don't worry it's fine, c'mon."

"I don't want to."

It didn't matter.

My tears kept pouring.

"I don't want to, I don't want to, I don't want to."

My brain was frozen. *If I fight back and he still doesn't stop, can I live through that reality? Or is it easier to just stay silent, to suffer, to just let him ignore the fact that I said no? This way,* I thought, *at least it's my shame to carry.* I just didn't realize how long it would stay with me.

I became something, someone so different from what my friends and family knew. Someone who was hard for us all to recognize. Instead of being the girl who had so much light, all I mirrored was darkness and submission. The girl we used to know was not here anymore and it did not feel possible that we could ever get her back. The girl I became, was the girl who was too scared to say no, to rock the boat, too scared that the fear would swallow her whole. That it would take her innocence just like it did when she was little.

It was impossible to tell the truth. I could not tell my friends and family the truth because I knew that they would try to save me. I could not tell him the truth, because of his reactions towards me. And I could not tell myself the truth because if I were being honest with myself, I would be screaming at who I have become.

The person in the mirror was such a disappointment. The person in the mirror was me as a child.

I was convinced that my fear of him was love, it was passion. I was convinced that his asking and asking after every "no" was because he just loved me so much that he couldn't take "no" for an answer. Love was manipulation. Love was gas-lighting. Love was force. Love was drama. Love was pain. That is what I saw. That is what I learned. That is what I mimicked. But it was so very wrong.

Once I was able to group him into the same type of person that my stepfather was, my fear of him tripled. I am seeing things more clearly and it scares me as it always should have.

* * *

On May 26, the next morning after my birthday and after my dinner with my dad, I waited until Cody left for work. The second I heard that front door shut, I knew I only had a matter of hours to get out of this house. There was no time to pack my things up neatly. Since my dad hasn't been home for months, I have been staying here often to avoid being alone. I brought over my most needed things, from clothes and shoes to even my large make-up vanity. I tried to make somewhere feel like home. But it never would.

Once the door closes, I am in the closet and throwing everything I can into trash bags. I grab my hangers with the clothes still on them and run them out to my car. I sprint to the bathroom and slide one arm across the counter as my other hand holds open a grocery bag to catch all my things as they slide off.

I will leave without a note, without a goodbye, without a trace. I know that this is the only way I can leave since I have tried and failed to leave him in other ways before. I manage to get everything out except my vanity. Because no matter how hard I keep trying, there is no chance of me fitting my makeup vanity into my beloved car Karen. While I adore that two-door cherry red Pontiac G-6, she lacks room for storage, and I am running on borrowed time.

As I drove off, I realized I left my jewelry box behind too. It is not a huge deal in that I have nothing expensive inside. All my jewelry is cheap and can be replaced. Except for that locket. The locket from my deceased great-grandmother is in it. It was her gift to me before she passed. I knew the risk of leaving these items, but I didn't have time to make two trips before he got back. I would never see that locket again. *I am so sorry, great grandma.* I just couldn't risk it.

Giving Cody the opportunity to stop me was not something I was willing to do. As I drive home with my things, I feel free.

I knew I would have to go back to that apartment at least one more time. I had to get my vanity. The thought of going back felt even scarier than leaving the first time. I knew I had to go in fully armed. I needed to go in with my father.

"I am coming to get my vanity. My dad is with me. Can you leave the door unlocked?" I texted him.

I had to unblock his number to ask him for one last favor. Luckily, whatever messages he had been sending me since I left, never came through.

"Ya, I'll be gone in an hour" he replied.

Knowing he would let us come while he wasn't at home offered an abundant amount of relief. My dad had agreed to help me, but not because he knew I was scared. He didn't know that yet. But because he knew I needed his car to fit the vanity and his strength to lift it up.

Since Cody wouldn't be home to deliver his message, he made sure he left one behind for us. The humiliation I felt walking into that apartment with my father would bury me. The shock would hit first, then the envelope of embarrassment.

There were intentionally placed items like bras and other women's clothing slung all over my vanity. Empty beer cans were everywhere, all of which spilled onto my things. It was such a gallant attempt to hurt me one last time. But it didn't hurt in the way that he would expect. This is the type of behavior I expected from him, while shocking to see, I was not that surprised.

It was gross and it sucked to see all of my things trashed like that, but it also felt so reassuring. Like I was doing the right thing, for once. It had a unique effect on me. It stung a little, but mostly it just reiterated how messed up the whole situation was. It was a mess I was happy to be leaving.

My rose-colored glasses were finally yanked off and I could easily see that I was living a life that I never wanted in the first place. I was just ashamed that my father had to see that his daughter ever put up with someone like this. But as I walked out that door with my things, I left the shame and embarrassment behind. It truly was never mine to carry, it was his. I closed the door behind me. I knew I would never come back here.

* * *

It was hard to see at eighteen. At the time, I had no clue why or how I even got here, I just simply was here with no way out. I had no clue that I chased these men who reminded me of my stepfather because, in my brain's own twisted way, it was "safer" because it was known. I knew how to navigate this. I knew how to survive this. I had done it before.

Just like my mother, I tried to leave many times. Only to find myself falling back into the vortex like a spell of ignorance had taken over me. And just like my mother, the longer I stayed in it, the more dangerous it became. The repetition, while tragic, provided comfort. I knew what to expect. I have learned that the brain craves what it knows. Even if what it knows, is toxic.

Once I left, everything started to become abundantly clear. With each day of freedom, I became more aware of my issues. Without the high of survival, I was able to find awareness.

All of the puzzle pieces were finally in front of me, but with no guide on how to put them back together. I started to see that the issues in my behaviors, in my choices, in the things that kept on happening to me, were my responsibility to own. I wasn't a kid anymore, I needed to stop wailing "Why me" and find a way to move forward. I played an essential role in all of my problems. It became painfully clear to me that for the past few years, I took zero ownership of my life. I was just a floater, never wanting to take a risk or try anything new. I just followed my emotions and never stopped to think very rationally about anything. I was acting like a victim. Like I didn't have any choices. Like I was sleepwalking through my own life because the only thing worse than feeling nothing at all would be feeling everything all at once.

It took so much of me to get out of these habits. It wasn't until that final figurative and literal shove, that I even became aware of it, that I even woke up. The fights were growing with intensity and getting out of control. The yelling, the chasing, and finally the feeling of his hands on my shoulders shoving me against the wall, the frame, the glass shattering on the floor and the look in his eyes when I finally got up. It was at that moment that I saw exactly where my life was headed and the voice in my head screamed, "Run."

And for the first time, my voice was heard.

Chapter 3:
Setting Boundaries

Our past wounds have a tendency to fester. They grow on us and left untreated they can lead us into darkness, disaster, chaos, and depression. But if we are willing to look inside, to go into the darkest rooms in our hearts, we can find understanding, awareness, and acceptance that we never had before. That is where we find ourselves, buried under the pain in the rooms.

A lot of my young life was spent burying all the things that had happened to me. Partly because I felt like I could never talk about them, if I told someone else, it would make it real and there would be risks in admitting the truth. The other reason

I hid them was because I felt stupid for how sad I was feeling. I felt like it was unjustified. I had been told so often "Don't be dramatic" or "it could always be worse." It was hard not to hear those voices because I felt like in comparison with so many others, I was way better off. I mean, so many people had it way worse than I did, so what gave me the right to feel so low? I had a good life, a happy one even, and I was fortunate in so many ways. So why was I struggling so much? And more importantly, why did I feel so guilty to admit that I was struggling?

These were some of the very first questions I had when I started therapy. Why was I in so much pain? And why did I feel stupid for it? Why did I have this undying feeling that I had to prove that what I went through was enough to justify my level of sadness? In response, my therapist asked a quite simple, yet totally logical question,

"Do you think it hurts when you break your leg?"

"Well, yeah," I thought, kind of confused about where this was going.

"Do you think that a broken leg makes it hurt any less if you stub your toe?" she answered.

I took a second to think about this concept. That pain truly is not something to be compared, it is something to be felt. While clearly, anyone understands a broken bone is worse than a stubbed toe, they both hurt. That's what mattered. The hurt.

As simple as the phrase was, it made total sense to me. What mattered was not the actual events. I was not an objective judge on those anyway. After all, I was not in competition with anyone else, what mattered was the feelings that came out of it. I had to accept that I was in pain, and regardless of what caused it, I needed to address it in order to move forward in my life. Pain is not something that can be buried or stored inside, it always finds somewhere to let itself out and if we don't make the first move on it, we can lose control. That's how it was for me.

The next questions I had directly stemmed from my relationship troubles.

"Why was I with someone who treated me like that?"

"Why did I stay so long? Why did I feel like I couldn't leave?"

"How did I not see the truth that everyone else seemed to?"

"How did I allow myself to get so lost? So low?"

"What the heck is wrong with me?"

She responded with a question, "Do you think you even knew who you were at that point in your life? Perhaps you lost yourself because you didn't really know who you were yet."

That seemed fair, I thought. I have been struggling since I was twelve and by the time I turned eighteen I was dying for an identity, specifically one that was the opposite of who I was now. It was a fair assumption.

"Yeah, I guess I didn't. I guess I don't know who I am yet,

but I know that this is not who I want to be" I respond.

This couch does that to me. It hugs me with security and it's easy to be vulnerable. My therapist responds with a smile. The kind of smile that makes me feel understood. I had come here to change, and she was ready and willing to help me do that.

"We need to do some searching, find out what is in your unconscious. All of those things have a heavy imprint on your behavior. We will need to explore those more to understand what led you here."

She went on to show me a picture of an iceberg. It was a beautiful metaphor for humans. What people see on the outside is so small and minuscule compared to the gigantic mass that lies underneath the surface. I knew exactly what she meant. The things I had been through, had shaped and influenced who I had become. I needed to understand them, so I could get control of my life back. I needed to understand me. To be true to me.

Before we could dive in, for what I assume was a goal for my safety, we talked about how I could start setting boundaries. We talked a lot about how my boundaries, or lack thereof, were way too far back. She compared them to a line in the sand. Something we could move, something we could always change.

"Let us find a place where you feel like your boundaries should be in a relationship. What are the things you absolutely do not want to tolerate?" She asked me.

I started rattling off my list of nonnegotiable behaviors.

That seemed easy enough until I realized that all my nonnegotiable behaviors were things that my ex did to me. Things that I watched my stepfather do to my mom. The pattern couldn't be ignored. At least now, I knew I would never stick around for any of these things again. I finally knew what I wanted to tolerate and I had clear boundaries in place to ensure that was the case.

Without these limits, forgiveness for unforgivable actions was dished out in plenty. I finally understood the necessity of having rules and boundaries in my life, especially when it came to relationships. These things exist for our protection and they were something I was finally going to learn how to have. I wasn't going to tolerate infidelity or abuse any longer or ever again.

My therapist and I decided it would be best to start off meeting once a week, there was a lot to unpack and get through and it was going to take some time. My parents generously agreed to help me pay for it, there was no way I could afford therapy working part-time at a salon. I was new to doing hair and was in the beginning phases of building my clientele. All my money went to therapy, rent, and whatever food I could afford afterward. Often, it was ramen noodles. Because they were only a couple of dollars and they were delicious. Ramen noodles and coffee became my diet of success.

I agreed to be completely sober during my time in therapy. It was something we talked about right away. It was crucial to my well-being that I was completely present in this process and not using anything that would compress my true feelings down.

This was easier than I expected. Turns out, when I left my ex, I didn't feel like I needed a substance to help me escape anymore. I already had.

I got sober instantly, it was easy, I wasn't addicted to any substance, but I was drinking too much. The only hard part about being sober is that you become so aware. I started to really see how badly this all affected me. I made the worst decisions when I was drinking. I created so many of my own problems, and that was hard to admit. It's easy to have a bad guy, to have someone else to blame, but what if so much of what went wrong, was my own doing? I had to get prepared to live with this.

My goal in going to therapy was just to get better. I wanted her to fix me. Like any other doctor, I made the naive assumption that simply going to therapy could cure me. I found out quickly that I was wrong. That only I, with my therapist's help, could do that. Nothing that was done, could be undone. But I could be better for it, I could change my perspective, my behaviors, and my inner thoughts, all of which would make me better. But the past would stay. The past is not a stain you can scrub out. A magic eraser couldn't even tackle that job.

I made some rules for myself as I began my journey back in time. The first was that I was going to be upfront and honest about the way I felt. Even if it made me feel crazy. I was dying to live in a world where there was no need or obligation to justify emotions, but instead to just feel them. So, I decided that for myself, this therapist's room would become that world.

I spent my entire young life trying to justify why I was so incredibly sad. Trying to make sense of it. And now I finally could. Without understanding, the emotions made me feel like I was super alone, or something was seriously wrong with me. I was aching to come up with some reason for those big feelings because many people had it worse than me and they seemed to be doing just fine. So, why wasn't I? I needed the answers. I craved them.

I felt weak, ashamed, and lost. I refused to tell anyone what was going on with me because I didn't understand it myself, so surely no one else would understand either. Except for now, maybe someone would. If only I had known that the whole time I spent trying to make sense of things, I just needed to accept that what happened in my life had happened. And that those events caused huge emotional impacts for me and that was my truth. No one needed to agree with me on that fact. Those events happened and I experienced great suffering because of it. Justification was never needed, but acceptance was.

The next rule I made was that I truly did not have any power over what I felt, but I have all the power when it comes to what I do. So, my therapist would help me navigate my emotions.

She would help me find the why, the how, and the healing. And for my actions? That was on me. I had to fix who I was to get the life I wanted.

My mother always told me, "Never let your memories be greater than your dreams" and this phrase inspired me to fight through the trenches. It meant so much to me, and it is my forever reminder that the past does not have to define who you become. Our memories shape us, yes. But our memories are not all that we are, they are simply our past and truthfully many of them do not belong in our futures. There is always hope for more.

In the clean-up of this room, I had to learn that drama is not love. That abuse is not love. And that what my brain knew was wrong and what was actually wrong were two vastly different things that needed updating. I needed to redraw my lines on what was acceptable in a relationship. I went from zero boundaries to concrete walls of protection and neither one of those options was going to work for me, for anyone.

I needed to see that real love is safe and a beautiful calm. It can even be the best type of boring and that was an incredible thing. I had to rewire my brain to learn that no matter what happened to me when I was a kid, it didn't have to control who I was or limit who I became. I could be more. I could have more. My mother could go on to have more, she deserves so much more. We all do.

Chapter 4:
Familiar Patterns

I walk into my therapist's office a nervous wreck. As I sit here on this couch, I feel the dread move up from my feet, into my legs, it grips my core and gets stuck in my throat. The tears are full and ready, feeling like a weight that my eyelids are struggling to hold back. *Just relax*, I remind myself.

I had been in therapy for a while now and it was finally time to start tackling some tough projects. It was time to step into the second room. I grabbed the box of tissues because I knew that this room would require a lot of tears from me, and I spent the first five minutes pretending like I had nothing to talk about. I was trying to avoid opening that door. My therapist saw right through it. She had many strategies that helped me listen and tune into myself and what I was feeling. This was easier than just being asked questions because instead of me searching for words to say, we were just following the feelings and seeing where we ended up.

"How do you feel?" she asked me.

"I'm okay," I said, offering little to nothing.

"Okay, well how about you close your eyes and take a minute to just tune into that okay. We will see what comes up" she replied.

I put my shaking hands on my knees and closed my eyes. *I don't want to go in here*, my gut screamed. The room I decided to step into terrified me, after all. I hadn't been there since middle school. But I felt like I should tackle this beast before moving on to other parts of my timeline. I remembered this time of my life the way you remember a nightmare. There were pieces missing, there had to be. It gave me that horrendous feeling like when you slightly wake up in the middle of the night from a bad dream and you are so exhausted that you know you have to go back to sleep, but you beg your brain to change the channel. Please don't take me back there, my mind and body beg me. Fear clouds so many of my memories from this time because it was the first time in my life that I felt threatened.

As I open the heavy wooden door, the eerie quiet greets me. There are no neighbors close by, no one to hear the screams. The outside view is gorgeous and the house smells like freshly cut wood. The dead animal heads on the walls aren't really my thing, but hey that's not why we're here. We are in this room because it has been haunting me for far too long and it is time to clean it up.

My mother took on the brave task of raising five children as a single mother and her search for love led us here. I was her baby, the youngest of five kids. This meant that by the time we got to this room, only one other sibling still lived at home with me and my mom and that was my older brother, Scott. We started living with our stepdad when I was eleven and Scott was fifteen. My mom and my stepdad were either madly in love or screaming at each other. Half the time I couldn't tell you which one was worse.

The house was full of odd rules, a much tighter ship than we were used to. One of them was that we could not go into the living room because that was his "man-room.'" Luckily for me, I was the type of kid who would rather hide out in my room anyway, an introvert through and through.

"Ash! Guess what?" My mom said as she opened my door to ask me. I looked up from my journal as I sat on my very emo bedspread. Yes, this was during my emo phase.

"He is going to be working out of town for a month" she cheered.

I couldn't believe it. I got off my bed and grabbed my journal and we both headed for that forbidden room. My mom could not stop smiling, she looked beautiful, and she looked free. We walked in and felt the brand-new carpet on our feet. I can't remember if it was actually new, or if it just felt new because no one was allowed to walk on it. We sat down and let ourselves sink into the big brown and inviting couch. It held us firmly as it was hardly ever used. We felt ridiculously cool to be sitting in this room, like we had won for the first time, in a long time.

I looked up at her and I asked the daunting question. The one I knew would kill the mood, but the one I knew had to be asked, "What happens when he comes home?"

"It will be better this time," she said insecurely.

We got word that he was headed back early from his trip, and my mom began psychotically cleaning every room. I watched her as she made sure there was not a single trace of anything left behind that might set him off. The fear in my mom's voice and actions told me so much more than I needed to know. She was trying to protect me as well as herself, but I was smart enough to see how frantically she picked that house up and made sure everything was perfect before he arrived. The longer I watched her, the angrier I became. So, instead of helping her, I went into my room, shut the door, and wrote in my journal about how much I hated all of this.

Then I heard the boasting voice, the loud footsteps, and within seconds the entire house changed from a home to a prison. I instantly regained the feeling that every step I took in this house felt like walking on ground that was waiting to crack. I watched as he stepped through the entryway and just before he could see it, my mother scooped up a pile of dog poop with her bare hands and shoved it into her robe pocket. If I didn't know how scared she was of him, this would have shocked me, grossed me out even, but I knew better. I knew she did what she did, because she didn't have any other choice. She just did what she did to protect our dog and to protect us. To avoid a fight by any means possible. We were willing to do a lot to avoid his wrath these days.

Tonight, was no different. The way the house was set up, my room was only one long hallway away from theirs. Meaning that every time they got into a fight like tonight, I could hear every word.

The sound was loud and stumbly. I heard a crash, a drop and screaming. The louder it got, the more scared I became. I peeked my head out of my bedroom door and saw him standing there on the ladder. My stepfather was standing at the top, working on something at the end of the hall, in his right hand he was holding a massive black wrench, and on his face a conniving smile.

I watched as my mother came out of the laundry room,

"What the hell was that for?" she yelled at him, neither one of them noticing me. "You shoved me into that dryer!" She followed as he didn't respond.

He laughed. Then he tilted his head back and kept his large dark eyes on her. His hand lifted up the wrench, "Oops, construction accident" he said as he threatened her.

"Don't you threaten me!" she screamed as she shook the ladder.

She's finally lost it, I thought, eyes wide and heart racing. *Is this how it ends?* I assumed it would end with one of them dead. I just didn't think it would be him.

My mother turned her back and saw me, "Get back in your room" she demanded. Even though she was attempting to shield me from this sight, I could see my mom's big brown help-me eyes. She couldn't hide her fear from me. We were too close. When she looked at me, I felt like I was supposed to do something, but I didn't. I froze. She shook the ladder in an attempt to stand up for herself, but what she found out, was that there would be no happy ending here.

She was terrified, I was terrorized, but I knew I couldn't call the police. I knew what could happen and that somehow seemed worse than surviving this. As soon as she stopped, he jumped down from that ladder and they went into their room to finish their fight. I guess she assumed if he was going to hurt her, at least this way I wouldn't have to see it.

What my mom doesn't know, was that as soon as that door shut, I snuck down the hall, tip-toeing my way down that cream-colored carpet until I reached the locked wooden door. I would slowly lower myself into a comfortable position because I knew I would be here for a while and I leaned in closely to make sure I could hear. I did this so many times. I would just sit and listen to make sure that she was safe. I pressed my ear against it and all I heard was yelling, swearing, and then crying. The noises began to settle, so I assumed the worst was over and she was safe. At least, for tonight. So, I pushed myself up and crept back to my room.

I never knew what was going on in there, but I was con-vinced that if I sat there, nothing too terrible would happen to my mom. I spent a lot of nights crying outside that door, counting down the days until he would ship himself off back to work again so I could catch a glimpse of the woman my mother used to be. Sometimes, like many toxic relationships, it would be incredible when he came home. He would be happy and kind. He would teach me how to fish and take me on spontaneous adventures, and in those moments, I could see a glimpse of what my mother saw in him. Those moments, while beautiful, were still outweighed by the violence and the fear he instilled. Because just as I have those memories, I still struggle to forget the other ones. Every happy moment was clouded by a scar.

* * *

My stepfather walks in after a long night of drinking in the barn by himself. He walks in heavily and clumsily all at the same time. His face is so red, his eyes burning, and his brows furrowed. I watch him carefully as he stumbles in, trying to gauge what could have set him off this time. I have seen this play out in many forms, so I try to mentally prepare for his reaction. His eyes glance right past us, but then he sees my mother on the couch.

My oldest brother Ryan and his girlfriend are over for dinner tonight. We didn't want things to end right after we ate, so they decided to stay a while to sit around and talk. My family loves to talk and with us five siblings, there is always an entertaining story. Many of which Ryan is the center of. He knows how to stir things up. How to cause trouble and how to keep us on our toes. As we sit and laugh, I watch how Ryan and his girlfriend are not fazed by my stepfathers' entry, but as for my mom and I, we watch him with caution.

As he gets closer, he steps and quickly kicks his boot off at my mother. I watch as it flies through the air and it just grazes her cheek. This sends him into a rage of lonely laughter. Ryan and his girlfriend are wide-eyed, and they look at me in search of the appropriate response. They don't realize, this is pretty normal around here.

I watch as they look at each other and then at the floor. They chose, no response at all. My mom's eyes are full of tears that she refuses to let fall. I roll my eyes, go to my room and slam the door. I am not even shocked and that's the problem. I am just so angry. Not with my brother or his girlfriend, not even with my mom, just at the pure fact that this situation is so messed up. At the fact that so many people are choosing to look the other way as they watch us tolerate this.

I don't know if my mom stood up for herself or not that night, I don't know if anyone said anything at all. I didn't wait that long. I couldn't. All I heard was my brother say goodbye to my door.

"Bye Chicken" his whisper hit me in the gut.

I didn't respond. He was hoping that his little nickname for me, the nicer one, would lighten the mood. It didn't. A tear carefully slid down my cheek. I didn't feel like I was a little chicken anymore. I sat by my bedroom window, pulled back the blinds and I watched him and his girlfriend drive away. I had the perfect view of the driveway from here. It had to be the longest gravel driveway I had ever seen, and at night when people drove away all you could see was their lights. It was so dark out here. The kind of dark that came from having little to no neighbors. The kind that came from having little to no hope. But watching those lights all I could feel was how jealous I was. If only I could just leave in these moments, if only it was that easy for my mom and I to get out.

"Take me with you" I cried out my window.

* * *

These random acts of intimidation are limitless. The longer we live here the intensity of the events slowly but surely increases. The longer we stay in this house, the more danger we are in.

Eventually, it became too much for my brother Scott and he decided to move in with my dad. He knew in his heart that the only ending here was destruction. As I watched him pack up to leave, my fear began to outgrow my body. He was the only safe and stable thing I had. I was going to be in this alone.

I could have gone with him, my mom even suggested it, but just until she got out, she reminded me. But how could I? I was insanely connected to my mom, it felt like we were one. Like leaving her behind, was leaving a part of me. I could not do it. So, I would bare what was to come. I would carry it with me forever, just to keep her safe. I had this perspective that I had to stay here with my mom to keep her safe. I was a scrawny seventh grader, I knew in my heart there wasn't a whole lot I could do, but if he was going to hurt her, at least she wouldn't have to hurt alone.

The night before Scott decided to leave was soundless. He was in his room, and I was in mine. My mother and my stepfather were in the main house talking, but for once we couldn't hear a thing. They both had voices that carried, so this was weird even when things were good. The silence was broken instantly and without warning.

The sounds of moving furniture, running footsteps, and deep yells began to burst out. The mental war in my brain flew into full force. Should I open my door? What will I see if I do? Should I just pretend not to hear it? Should I hide? Maybe I should lock myself in and call the cops, but then, what would happen to me?

My mom would be so upset with me. There were too many unknowns, and the voices were only getting louder, louder. I couldn't hear myself over them anymore, my logical thinking began to shut itself down and all I could think was, survive. The guilt of this night would follow me into my adult life. I should have done something, should have called someone, anyone for help, I was frozen.

The sounds of things banging around echoed and the noises wouldn't stop. It sounded like an earthquake was just outside my door, shaking down the house around me. Then, I heard it. The deep, mellow yet somehow still commanding tone. It was Scott's voice, he was out there. Now there was no question, no time for freezing up because if he goes, I go too. A ship that cannot leave her dock. I could do this. I barely and silently opened my door, without anyone even glancing back to notice.

I could see just parts of her crying face, her long, blonde hair was messily tossed around in front of it. Her hands were on his wrists, losing color from her tight grip, trying to force my stepdad's large and beat-up hands back away from her neck. Her back was against that stupid stainless-steel fridge. He was so pissed off about that fridge. He was convinced we somehow dented it. And here he was, slamming her against it. Her once strong and beautiful face was full of horror and despair.

She looked unrecognizable to me. My mother would never allow this. I pushed the door open a little further, I watched my stepdad lower her and let her go. She slumped to the ground like a broken body. He only stopped because of Scott's yell.

He moved on from her and he chose a new face to scream at. But this one, wouldn't be bullied and wouldn't back down. That is not in his blood, it didn't use to be in my mom's either. It was at that moment, when he yelled at my brother, that I finally saw my mom again for who she was, who she used to be. She threw herself between them. By the look in her eyes, I knew he would have to kill her to get to my brother. He knew it too. There. She. Was. The mom I know her to be.

It was then, that Scott looked over and saw me peeking out, he backed up and shut the door in my face as an aide of protection, and screamed at my mother, "You may want to put up with this, but I don't have to!"

I knew right away that those words would cut her like a knife. I felt stuck in this moment, I was proud of Scott for finally saying something, but I was so afraid of what this meant for Mom and me.

But he was my brother. It was never his job to protect me. He just always did. No one said a word the rest of the night. No one came in to check on me, to explain, to apologize. Everyone went to their own rooms like everything was fine, and in the morning my brother left, and he never came back.

As long as my mother stayed, this house would continue to swallow me. I lay in bed and let my thoughts continue to grow my worries. Without Scott here, who would defend us now? Time crept by slowly after this day. Each day felt like a year. We learned to keep our heads down to avoid conflict. We learned to not rock the boat, to obey, to lay low, and to try and go unnoticed. These habits would follow me long after middle school. I would avoid any conflict at any cost.

For today, I had seen enough. I forced that heavy wooden door shut. It would take the strength of both of my hands. And then I took the breath I was struggling for. The peace offering of thinking back in time is that you have the choice of when to stop the story. I was done for now, at least for today.

"I'll be back for more tomorrow," I told my therapist as I walked out.

Chapter 5: Stay or Go

After a night off, I am ready. I am prepared to go back in. I have my guard up, but my heart is open and I know that if I keep fighting through it, I will find what I am looking for in this room. Understanding and forgiveness.

I sit in therapy hands grabbing my knees. I tap my long fingers against them and I close my eyes to tune in. The wooden door awaits me. I place my hand on the iron handle, I push it forwards and when I open my eyes, I am here.

The first thing that I notice is the pivot between my mom and my roles. They are beginning to change the longer we stay here. Instead of having me crying outside her door, she is crying outside of mine. The protector or so I thought, became the protected. Turns out, she was starting to fear him like I always did. Enough so, that she began to make plans to make sure he could never get to me again. This newfound protection should have made me feel safe, but it scared me even more. Why would she have to do that? I would often wonder. What is she trying to prevent?

What am I choosing to forget?

I am sound asleep in my bed when I am shaken and woken up. I feel unfamiliar hands on me, silently, but aggressively ensuring that I get out of bed. It was the middle of the night. I check my phone, it is three in the morning. All I can think, is why are you in here and what do you want from me?

"Get up and get dressed," my stepfather tells me.

I know better than to argue, I quickly slip on some sweatpants and a sweatshirt that my dad had bought me for my birthday from Pink last year. I love Pink, it makes me feel so grown up and so dang cool. My dad always gets me the best gifts. My dad. I metaphorically hang on to him as I walk back through this memory. As I struggle to feel safe. While my logical brain knows it can't hurt me, my body isn't responding that way. The goosebumps on my skin, the knot in my throat, and the tears in my eyes remind me, that I am still afraid.

"We're going to walk down to the pond to look for coyotes" my stepdad whispers to me.

He grabs his shotgun out of the safe and then he leaves it open. I notice this because he never leaves his safe open. I have never seen what's inside. Turns out, it's just a lot of guns.

We make our way down the path. It is not too long of a walk from our house down to the river. The property sits at the top of a hill and on the backside, you can walk down the path until you are greeted by the beautiful and unforgiving Colorado River.

Our property paves a perfect curved shape that directly backs up to the water. It's a dirt and gravel path, one I often enjoyed walking in the summers. My favorite part about it was when the river water was high, it would overflow and flood the dirt. It created the thickest, murkiest of mud you could imagine and it was so much fun to ride my Go-Kart through. These were the memories I tried to think of as we walked down to the pond. Myself, wild, free, and filthy from the mud.

As we were walking, he was charming and funny like he sometimes was. I knew better than to get my hopes up, but in these moments, I could see why my mom could love someone like this. He could be great sometimes, and as he smiled at me, I tried to feel calm.

"We'll stop here," he said as we got to the wooden dock. The wood was old, but the dock was stable. How symbolic, I thought. Chills began to cover my entire body, but I wasn't cold. Now that we were here, *what was going to happen?* I knew I should be afraid because he wasn't smiling at me now and he wasn't saying anything either. The cold night air was crisp and it settled over me with a warning. Everything in my body is saying, *run*. But my mind knows that I can't. So, it does what it can, it takes me out of the moment and to another memory.

My mind immediately took me out of this memory and far away from him. It did this sometimes, it was something that started happening when we moved in here. My brain would pluck me out of the moment and place me in a happier one.

I never really spent much time on this dock, so there wasn't a lot to pick from. So, I just dove into the first one that came to me, I could see my feet jumping into the little paddle boat I sometimes used. My lifelong friend Leah was there. We decided we would take the boat out and we would attempt to catch some fish. Every time I am on this dock, I can see us both panicking in that boat trying to decide what to do with the fish we just caught. We felt too bad trying to kill it, but we were too grossed out to touch it to try and get it off the hook. Poor planning on our part. She slightly smacked the fish's head with a rock trying to end it quickly. It was definitely not hard enough so we ended up just sticking the pole back in the water and prayed it would set itself free. Eventually, the little guy figured it out and I still feel bad that we probably left him with some brain damage.

I am pulled back into reality by his voice.

"Keep an eye out now, will ya?" he says to me.

I look at him and nod. I assume he means we are looking for coyotes, but I barely even know what they look like. I am just staring into the black, hoping my mom wakes up and notices that I am gone.

We stand here quietly for what feels like hours. I am exhausted and incredibly confused. I am not an extremely outdoorsy kid, I like to be outside, but I have zero interest in anything involving guns and animals. I can barely go camping because of the pure disgust that bugs bring me. It truly makes no sense as to why he would wake me up for this. The more I think about it, the more wrong it feels.

Maybe this was some weird type of punishment. He knows if he shoots an animal in front of me all it is going to do is make me cry a whole lot of tears. I am way too sensitive for hunting. I have no clue why he would wake me up for this, but I also am way too scared to ask why I am here. I suppose we're just going to sit here and stare into the night until he sees a coyote or something else to shoot. I have no clue. I have never touched a gun in my life, I was not raised around this stuff. I was a sheltered kid, until now.

After what I assume was an hour passed, a scream comes from our house. It is not just a yell or a scream. It is something more, like a fearful, painful, begging for help kind of noise. Immediately after the scream, a shadowy figure starts running from the house. My whole-body tenses and I press my hands into the wooden dock to bring myself to my feet. For a moment, I wonder if I should run. I watch as closely as I can through the pitch-black darkness, and I see that it gets closer down the path, with every quick stride. It is running, frantically, like prey when chased by a predator down the dirt path headed right for us. Was the coyote close by? Surely not this close.

As the figure gets closer, I can see it begin to take human form. I can barely make out the rocks flying from underneath her feet. It is my mother, and she looks horrified, screaming things.

"Get away from her!"

"If you touch her, I will kill you, I swear to God."

Now, I am even more confused and afraid. Why does she think he's going to hurt me?

The second she makes it to the dock, she throws her hands toward me and grabs me as hard as she can. She pulls me as far away from him as possible but remains close enough to be heard.

She had never handled me so roughly before. She puts herself between us and continues to shout. All I hear is noise, all I feel is shaking. My mind is blocking out so many words. It is like I am not even here, like I am watching this happen to someone else. I do that so frequently here. I imagine any other reality, other than my own.

My mom wraps her arms around me again and squeezes. She is holding me so tightly that I can feel her perfectly manicured, French-tip nails digging into my shoulders. I can feel her shaking body under my embrace and I can hear her whispering, thanking God that I am still here, like she almost lost me.

It is hard for me to process what is going on at this moment, but what I do know, was that for the first time in a long time, I felt like we were going to be okay. My mom finally loosens her grip after a few minutes, but not entirely, she takes me under her arm and walks me back up to the house. We are walking quickly and without a word and when we get to the backdoor, she kisses my cheek.

"Go to bed and lock the door. I love you" she says.

"Okay, mom. I love you too."

I walk to my room, lock the door behind me, get into bed, and do what I am told. But as I lay here, I can't help but wonder what in the hell just happened. I lay back and let myself relax and as my head hits the pillow I hear something heavy sliding across the floor, it sounds massive, steady, and extremely close to my room. And then I hear a *thump*. Something just slightly hit my door, I decide that whatever it is, it can wait until morning.

The morning sunrise greets me through my window, I wake up slowly as I often do. The light makes it impossible to sleep in. I am severely disappointed by the lack of sleep from being out all night. But I roll out of bed in hopes of being greeted with coffee, the one thing that will help me feel better. I have been drinking it daily since I was nine.

I open my door to make my way to the kitchen but immediately see that I am blocked in. The big heavy object I heard last night, is the old, forest-green, futon that goes with our couch. And the thing that hit my door, is my mother's sleeping body. She slept here, I realize. She pushed that giant futon in front of my bedroom door and she slept here. And from this night to our very last in this house, I would hear her slide it over and go to sleep and do the same. The protective mother I had once known, was slowly, but surely making her way back to me. Here she was sleeping in front of my door with no explanation other than she wanted to keep me safe. All I wanted to do, was beg her to let us leave and I did relentlessly. While this was a great step in the right direction, the best step would be one taken outside of this prison.

Eventually, she told me it was because that night before they went to bed, he had told her,

"I can do anything I want to that girl and there is nothing you can do to stop it."

But she wouldn't tell me this until six years later.

The whole couch guard dog thing could not last forever, so after that night, we waited him out until he left town for work again. This time, instead of relishing in our temporary freedom, we packed our things like maniacs to get the heck out of there. We didn't have anywhere to go, but my overly sweet coffee-breathed art teacher had something modest for us to live in until we could figure it out.

The house, if you could call it that, was a shed-like building with one bedroom and lots of mice occupying it. Aside from the one bedroom, which my mother generously gave to me, there was a large closet that she turned into a room for herself. She felt so terrible that we had to stay here, so she thought that giving me the bedroom was one way she could make it better. What she didn't know, was that I was so damn happy to be in any house other than the one we just left. It wouldn't have mattered if it was a tent. I just wanted out. I just wanted peace. This tiny house, as small and as filthy as it was, gave me that. It embodied a sense of safety that I hadn't felt in a long time. For me, it was symbolic. It was the picture of my mom choosing us and our safety and our happiness over the man she once loved. It was a home. And that was something I hadn't had in years. But home wouldn't last long because that would be too easy.

My new bedroom had a beautiful bay window that looked out to the street. This tiny little yellow-chip-paint house was built with this incredibly perfect space for me to sit and read. It could have been made special for me. It couldn't have been better. Maybe my art teacher knew I would love it and during the day, I did. But at night, this peaceful sanctuary quickly became a tunnel of nightmarish thoughts as soon as the sun went down and the world went dark. Staring out the window during the day, I would feel peace and hope for the future. I would dream of what good things could come and I was ready to greet them graciously. But, at night, when the dark came as it always does, I would find myself filled with angst and worry, *what if he finds us here?*

These worries and these thoughts often led to bad dreams, hearing that truck engine roar as it pulls up into our driveway to take us back to hell itself. I dreamed of it, feared it, hallucinated it, heard it and then lived it.

But the night before we went back, was one I cannot forget. Perhaps because I have so many memories like this. My mom means everything to me, and growing up there was no one I loved as much as I loved her. She always smelled the same. Her *Beautiful* perfume that came in that gold bottle always radiated off her flawlessly. That scent brings me comfort even in the worst of times. Growing up there was nothing better than sitting on her lap. I would lay my head on her chest as she rocked her chair back and forth. She would take her always perfectly manicured nails and run them through my hair as I cried and melted into her.

She has this way of making people feel completely safe and loved without bounds. Even if many times I never told her why, she would just let me be sad and rock me in that chair until I wasn't.

On this night, she knew why I was so upset. We were going back. She could not convince me of the why, she just told me that we were. I felt betrayed, I felt angry, but I was still desperate for her to make me feel like we were going to be okay. Neither one of us had words. So instead of talking about it, she rocked me in that chair. I held onto her like she was life itself and I let myself settle into that Beautiful perfume, I inhaled it and melted into her loving embrace, and as we rocked back and forth, I prayed that something would happen, anything at all, that would stop us from going back.

My prayers were going unanswered lately and my faith was shaking. In the morning, we went back to him and that house, just to move out and run away again. We did this three times, we went back, he hurt us more, we ran, we went back, and he hurt us worse, it was a never-ending cycle of punishment. Of fear. Of pain. Of trauma and life-long consequences. It would take years of therapy to sort it out. To accept it. To forgive and to understand. To cut him out of my life forever. And eventually, my mom would do the same, it would just take her longer. She would not get there until 2015.

But I would do this in the summer of 2008. I was done, even if she wasn't.

Chapter 6: The Cleanup

The best place to start healing is within yourself, but often times the world is too loud to even hear it. So, when I finally do give it a voice, it screams out with rage. My own voice had been silenced for so long, that it was dying to get out. Therapy ended up being a lot harder than I thought.

The many issues I struggle with today, I inherited from this time period in my life. Not only because they were so incredibly hard at the time, but because in a weird way, they set me up to chase these toxic patterns for years to come. The irrational fears, the fight or flight, the constant worry of never truly being safe. Those things were here to stay. The anxiety with loud noises, with yelling, with the dark. The habit of walking around on eggshells, the fear of speaking up, of disturbing the peace, of being honest, of being heard. These started to wash over me. These fears seemed like they would have led me into a life of calmness, of safety, but they didn't. They buried me in an abusive relationship.

The brain somehow chases what it knows, even if what it knows is toxic and terrifying. The relationships I chased as I grew up, mimicked patterns much like the ones I saw in my mother and step-fathers. The relationship I never wanted was the one I kept blindly walking into. Because even though I knew what I wanted and it wasn't this, I was attracted to what I knew how to deal with, which was abuse. In my messed-up way, I was comfortable because it was a "known" and "normal" thing. It was what I knew how to deal with. I knew how to survive, so I did.

I did not have to chase what I saw, I could change myself and in turn, my life would follow. I could choose to love myself.

It took me a long time, and I am still working on it, but I am learning and accepting that none of the things that happened in that house were my fault. I was only a child. I am still trying to convince myself that none of those things said anything about my worth, my value, or what I deserved. Most of the time, I have that part mastered, but every now and then, those same old insecurities come out. The shame of mimicking my past instead of learning from it comes out. But eventually, I learned. That's what matters most.

My goal is to constantly work on these issues. To constantly remind myself that they didn't make me wrong, broken, or messed up. But they made me strong, compassionate, resilient, and better than I was before. I had to accept that during this time, I had zero control. Which is why I love being in control now, over everything. It drives the people I love crazy. However, they know where it's coming from and they help me through it. Working on myself tends to be a recursive thing because I am never truly finished. I just have to keep updating myself, keep trying, and keep putting in the work to be better than I was yesterday. The first steps for me were to accept and forgive.

Luckily, when I was ready to talk about all of this with my mom as an adult, she made me feel acknowledged and heard. Hearing her side, woman to woman, provided me with so much healing. Especially because by the time we talked it out, I had already dated someone so similar. At that moment, the forgive-ness began to sink in. I could see that she was just as scared and as lost as I was. And if I needed any help in understanding her and the decisions she made, my own relationship gave it to me. This room helped me understand myself. It helped me forgive myself. It helped me forgive my mother. I no longer felt disgust and shame here, I felt empathy for little me, understanding for teenage me, and acceptance for adult me. It was finally time to walk out, the room was clean.

Chapter 7: Unexpected

I walk in today, ready. I position myself comfortably on my therapist's couch as she welcomes me.

"Can I get you anything to drink?" she offers me.

"I'm okay, thank you," I say as I fidget with the tissue box.

She glances at it in my hands, it's my fast and effortless way of telling her I am going to be crying in about .25 seconds. She smiles at me and we begin.

I am ready to go into this room today because honestly, I have never left it. I have yet to have that luxury.

This room has a revolving door that is constantly opening and closing. Constantly hurting, worrying, and somehow being kind of okay again. This room is not one I have escaped, nor will I ever, because it is a room I will constantly be walking in and out of.

I push the glass revolving door, the one that's lined with gold and worry, and I stop it just before I hit the hard stuff. I'll step out here.

It is July 7, 2011. I am seventeen years old, captain of my cheer team, and preparing to enter my senior year of high school. Three years have passed since we left my stepfather and I am finally beginning to feel safe again. My mother was able to find us a great house right up the street from my oldest brother Ryan's neighborhood. He is number one, while I am number five out of our siblings.

The street we lived on is called Bear Dance and I love that the stucco on the house is a warm brown color that mimics the hues and tones of a real teddy bear. It feels so fitting, so safe here. It is a tall two-story house shaped much like a square.

In this house, my mother and I get closer than ever. Every Monday night, when they release a new episode, we watch our show, *The Secret Life of an American Teenager*. It becomes our special thing. We will watch it together and it will encourage us to have so many important conversations that actually reflect so much of my own life as a high school girl. I tell my mom every-thing. Probably more than she wants or needs to know. But I know I can trust her with any secret, and I know I can come to her without judgment. This is something I hope to mimic with my own children when I someday become a mother, this unwavering, unconditional love. It is something my mother, my siblings, and I take so much pride in having.

Today, on July 7, 2011, I will witness this love and this fam-ily, be put to the test. To see if the power of our bonds is enough to get us through. I will finally step into the dark corners of this room, to the worst part about this day, because this is the day that my brother got his diagnosis. This is the day when I find out my brother has cancer. I hate this room and the revolving door that comes with it.

If there is one universal word that can bring anyone to their knees, it's cancer. That one word can entice a full-on panic from the patient and everyone who loves them. It's the one word that can forever change families and nothing will ever be the same. That's why life after cancer is so often referred to as the "new normal" because nothing actually goes back to the way it was before the illness. It can't.

As a college football player, the last words my big brother Scott thought he would hear was "You have cancer." It came for him out of nowhere, stealing much of his young life from him.

Scott was number four. He was the closest one to me in age out of my siblings and in so many ways, we were threaded so tightly together. He was the only one who shared a father with me. While all five of us shared our mom, Scott and I, had a dad of our own.

Before they found Scott's cancer, he was the one I counted on for everything. Because whether we were at our mom's or at our dad's, he was the one constant thing with me.

However, in 2010 that starts shifting. Scott suddenly starts going to multiple doctor's appointments for random things. He has a rash on his feet, they chalk it up to something simple and they prescribe a cream. Then, he is having trouble swallowing.

"How was your appointment?" I ask.

"The doctor thinks it is just my thyroid," he tells me over lunch.

I don't really know what that means, but I don't ask. He just keeps going to appointment after appointment, and they just keep missing it. Until we are in my dad's kitchen and he is trying to eat something small. I watch and notice quickly that the trouble he is having swallowing his food has intensely increased. This is not normal. It looks like his throat cannot fit down even the smallest bites of food. He almost chokes.

We assume it is nothing, or it is just some weird thyroid issue. No one thought for a second that it was a tumor. He is only twenty-one years old, we have no reason to. By the time the doctor finds it, almost an entire year later in 2011, the tumor is the size of a softball. It is taking up a ton of space in his throat and has been growing freely for who knows how long. Since it took so long to find it, it was progressing at a quick and aggressive rate.

I blink and I am at that doctor's appointment with my parents and him. We are here to find out what this tumor is, to do a biopsy. We all drive separately and we meet in the parking lot. As we all finish parking, we step out of our cars and walk into the large, brick building together. I take the first chair I see, I sit in the waiting room as my parents walk back with Scott for the appointment. Even though my parents haven't been together since Scott and I were toddlers, they know how to come together in times like this.

I sit in that chair for about an hour. I spend most of the time observing the sterile office. I never understand why these buildings look so grim and smell so terribly. The scent of bleach, with a hint of iron and vomit, consumes the air. The walls are blank just like the stare on the receptionist's face. *Can't they make these horrid places more inviting? Didn't everyone here know I was awaiting crucial news? Why must I panic alone out here?*

From a distance, I see my mother, father, and Scott in between the two of them walking out slowly. They are heading in my direction in slow strides. They both hold onto him in a way that seems like he needs to be held up. The procedure was minor, so the fact that he needed some help walking, meant that the news was bad enough to knock him off his exceptionally large feet.

As they get closer, I can see the look on their faces. I don't need them to tell me the results, their faces shout it out to me. I knew it, he has cancer. My mom's tears storm down her cheeks, my father can barely look at me, and Scott looks so far away. He is doing everything he can to mentally escape this moment like I often do.

"He has stage 2B Hodgkin's Lymphoma" my dad quietly says to me.

"It has spread to various parts of his body, and he will quickly begin chemo, radiation, and surgery. It's pretty bad Ash, but the doctors told us that it is curable, so we need to stay positive for him."

Stay positive, I say in my head. I don't know how to do that, but I try and I save the tears for the drive home. I save them for me. *At least I was positive in front of them*, I think.

The treatment plan starts almost instantly. They need to make up for lost time. When they do the full pet scan, they can see that the cancer has already spread, and he has multiple tumors throughout his body. He has surgery to remove the tumors they can and he immediately started chemo to kill the rest.

Once chemo begins, it doesn't take long for him to start mimicking the symptoms I have read about on Google or the ones I had seen on TV. Up to this point, the only experience I have with cancer come from watching *Grey's Anatomy*. Now I am going to learn about it on a personal level. His deep brown hair begins to fall out within weeks. It is something I knew to expect, something most cancer patients know to expect. It felt so frivolous to care about hair at a time like this, but I do. I am pissed he has to lose one more thing. Somehow, his bushy eyebrows that sit above his deep brown eyes, held on for dear life, they manage to stay on for most of it, but eventually, those fall out too. I am surprised there is a drug strong enough to take those things down.

The only thing that falls off his body faster than his hair is his weight. My brother is a big guy, he stands six feet, six inches tall. He weighs well over two-hundred pounds. He is tall and lengthy, and while he is definitely thin, he packs on a ton of muscle. He has no fat to lose. In some ways, I felt like his going in so strong and healthy was such a benefit, but it took little to no time for him to look gaunt and lifeless.

The color quickly began to drain from his once tan-olive skin. Our Italian complexion disappeared, as the chemo left him fair and almost purple and jaundiced. Little by little, I watch him look less and less like the brother I know. But the one thing he never loses is his strength. Not mentally, anyways. While his physical strength is shriveling down to almost nothing, his mind remains strong. And never once does he let us hear him complain.

He makes it through the first round of treatments in about six months. It blows me away to see how quickly he starts to bounce back to his old self once the chemo stops. I don't understand how he could present himself like he is so at peace, so quickly after winning this battle. The cancer is gone, yet he remains. He made it all the way to 2012.

* * *

I push the revolving door further. I am at my next stop. This door won't let me out after just one, it will continue to take me through all the painful parts of this room.

When I step out, it's warm. It is officially May, which means I am about to graduate high school. Finally. Thank God. Praise Jesus. It is over. This year was far from my favorite. A year that was supposed to be full of fun, was full of fear. I worried about my brother every single day, it was hard to allow space in my head for much else.

I got into every college I hoped for, only to turn them down and apply last minute to the smaller University in my hometown. The one I never wanted to go to. The one I refused to apply to. But as it got closer, I got cold feet. I was terrified to leave my family, I felt awful leaving Scott, and my boyfriend Cody (we were still together at the time) told me he would break up with me if I left. So, I stayed.

I try to keep my head up anyways. Scott's cancer's gone and the journey ahead is exciting and full of promise. I am eager to start college and even more eager to pursue a life as a therapist. That's my goal. I want to become a therapist and help as many people as I can. The other goal is to write a book about my life and my experiences, while I may be young to do this, as I am so often reminded, I feel that we all have a story worth telling, no matter our age. *I just want to help people, I just want to help me.* That was the motivation. To share, connect, and help. If it is true what they say, that one person's story is another person's survival guide- why wouldn't I share mine?

I am ready and willing to chase my dreams just like everyone else my age. *I just need to get through June first*, I remind myself. June marks my brother's six-month date of being in remission. This is the month when he will undergo another full-body PET scan to ensure that the cancer has not returned.

This waiting game is slow, yet fast, all at the same time. It is slow as in you feel like you are waiting for your doom, but it comes quick, like most unpleasant things do.

"Good luck today, Scotty. I love you. I'm here for you" I text him.

"Thanks. Love you too." He replies.

He is always so sweet in these moments like I am wishing him good luck on a date or something, not like I am wishing him good luck on his life.

Good luck, it feels so stupid. I never know what to say.

It feels like forever waiting for him to let me know what the results say. I compulsively check my phone every other minute while I wait.

"It's back" he sends me in a text. Nothing else. I am sure he is short on words.

Seconds after his text, my phone rings, *Mom*.

I can't hear words if she's saying any. Just loud, heavy sobs.

"Did your dad tell you?" she stumbles out.

"Not yet, but Scott di-."

"What did he tell you?" She interrupts me.

"Just that it's back, I don't know anything yet. I am so sorry, Mom."

She sobs. She can't talk anymore and I can't come up with anything helpful to say. Just as I try to comfort her, my phone rings again. "I'm sorry Mom, Dad's calling me. I will call you back, okay? I love you."

"I love you more" she cries into the phone.

The conversation with my dad is so different. He somehow

can always keep himself together, at least when he's talking to me. He tells me the facts, the things I need to know, the things to prepare for. He tells me these things in a matter of fact, analytical way.

Then he wraps it up with, "I know honey, it sucks. I love you."

"I love you more" pours out of me.

I hang up the phone, it falls from my hands, and I drop to my knees. Then, I scream.

I am forced to face the reality that I keep shoving down. I could lose my brother and there is nothing I can do to stop it. *I could lose my brother, but I can't lose my brother.*

Experiencing loss was a guarantee in this life, but it wasn't one I was comfortable thinking about at seventeen. I had never really been through it before. Other than losing great-grand-parents, which while hard, is expected. Losing a sibling this young is not.

The only real guarantee we have with this diagnosis is that we were going to watch Scott suffer. Which he does, terribly.

I am confused by the return of his cancer, because when he first got diagnosed, the doctor told our family verbatim, "If you have to get cancer, this is the one you want, it is generally very treatable."

He said it with such confidence that I used that statement as a seed of comfort through it all. I assumed the doctor told us this because it was true, and it provided hope. But at this moment, I felt like we had been lied to.

We were sold my brother's diagnosis in a package of both terrible disappointments, yet in a way that we should be grateful at the same time. Not everyone is so lucky to get diagnosed with treatable cancer if they are so unfortunate to get cancer in the first place. For Scott, the cancer was treatable. This part was absolutely true, he was treated after six long months, but now after six more, it has come back, even worse than before, were the odds still the same? Were they still on our side? It doesn't feel like they are anymore.

His cancer is extremely aggressive, persistent, and relentless. Much more than the doctors predicted it would be. He became such a complex case, that our small-town hospital just couldn't cut it anymore, so within a month or two he would be moving to Houston to receive treatment at one of the best research hospitals in the country, M.D. Anderson.

Luckily, our father is able to go with him. This is a luxury we know to appreciate. My father owns a local car dealership and his managers are kind enough to step up and take care of things while he is away. They know he is doing far more important things than work. We are all relieved that someone in the family can be with Scott full-time as he navigates this steep and ominous battle. At least, he won't be alone. Even though, in many ways, I felt like I would be. Without Scott here, I always feel lonely.

Almost two months have passed since Scott and my father moved to Texas for the treatment, the one his medical team called "The Stanford V." This treatment is known for being a more rigorous administered form of chemo. One that they use when the cancer phase of Hodgkin's Lymphoma is more advanced. One that would be so strong that while it was working to kill cancer, it sure looks like it is killing my brother too. He looks a lot worse this time around.

It is difficult to prepare for my first day of college when all I can think about is my brother. It is difficult because none of my friends are going with me. It feels like no one around me can relate to what I am going through and when I try to lean on Cody he is never there.

I am an introverted person and college terrifies me. There are going to be so many people and I will not know most of them.

I pull on a salmon-colored sundress and slip on some sandals, the first day-of-school outfit fad has still not outgrown me. It still feels important to have just the right thing to wear on the first day. I straighten my hair, which takes about an hour because of how long it is. I put on a ton of makeup, fake eyelashes, and the works. I spent almost two hours trying to look so insanely different from myself. To look like anyone else. To hide behind my reality.

When I get to the campus, I decide to park by a run-down sandwich shop across the street. The parking garage gives me the creeps because of the limitless amounts of scary movies I have watched with my siblings growing up. Terrible things always happen in parking garages. I smack the crosswalk button with a shaking hand and quickly cross the street. The campus feels huge to me compared to my small high school. My high school was as big as one of these buildings with less than a thousand kids, and now I was on this seemingly massive campus with my crap sense of direction. I have no clue where to go. It doesn't help that I refuse to ask anyone for directions.

After a few wrong turns, I finally am able to find my first building. The tall, tan-colored, brick building taunts me. I can make out the name from a distance. I let out a breath and pick up my pace. I know I am late to class and it is my number one pet peeve due to the attention it is going to draw to me.

I take the first empty seat and attempt to duck the spotlight as quickly as possible. Every word the teacher and the other students say comes out in a blur. As much as I hope my first year of college will be better than my last year of high school, I can't force myself to be present. My mind is always somewhere else.

My mind is a constant race of worry. Worrying about my brother and his cancer. Worrying about my boyfriend, worrying about doing anything he won't like. Worrying about myself and who I am becoming. I feel so broken and everything in my life feels so broken.

I jump out of the revolving door because it's left my head spinning enough for one day. I know there is more to face in this room.

Chapter 8: Not a Match

Six months came too fast and incredibly slow all at the same time. I do not know if there is anything more nerve-wracking than waiting to see if your cancer has remained gone or if it has chosen to come back to take more out of you. When the day came for Scott to get his scans, we as a family overwhelmed him with positive and hopeful messages encouraging him to "think best case scenario" or just a simple "I love you" in a small attempt to make him feel less alone.

The search for a bone marrow donor began. Time to try some-thing new, just chemo, surgery and radiation were not going to cut it.

"I am organizing a bone marrow drive," my mom said proudly to us. She found a way to help, and I could tell it felt good for her to find something in these moments that she could control. She texted us the information on it all. That way, even though I would not be getting tested here, I could still see the beautiful event that she orchestrated.

When I pulled up, I was overwhelmed by the turnout. It was incredible. It looked like there were hundreds of people lined up to be tested. We were officially in search of a match, for a way to save my brother. I decided not to stay, but I drove off with a smile. With hope.

The hospital had access to millions of donors on their own, but the problem was that there was not one single match from any one of them. And while my mother's attempt was honorable, it found matches for others, but it never found a match for Scott.

The next step was to look at the family. More specifically, me. My parents were not a match, but I, being his one full-blooded sibling, was the best hope according to his medical team. Our DNA is so closely aligned that the odds could be in our favor. I was our best hope.

With that, my parents told me I would be tested.

My father set up the appointment, and it was time for me to

do my part, time to see if there was anything I could do to save him. Getting my bone marrow tested came with overly complex emotions for me. I felt absolutely horrible and ashamed of my feelings of resistance, but in some ways, I prayed I wasn't a match.

It had nothing to do with not wanting to help, I wanted him to be saved with every ounce of my being, but it felt terrifying to be the one to do it.

Sometimes I would pray to trade him places, to take his suffering. It wasn't about selfishness. It had everything to do with, what if I am a match, I donate, and it doesn't work. I felt like I would own that failure and that I would never be able to live with it. The potential guilt felt haunting. My irrational thoughts convinced me that if my donation failed and something happened to him, my family would blame me. They wouldn't have, of course, but deep down, I know I would have owned that shortcoming as just another failure.

My father drove me to the appointment. The drive there was quiet and knowing my fears, he reminded me that "It is fine if you are not a match, but we just have to check."

We *have* to, I thought.

I knew he was trying to make me feel better, but I also knew that my entire family was banking on me being one. They said no pressure, but the pressure I felt was suffocating. I wanted to say no, simply because I feel like I never get to.

My dad held my hand while they drew tube after tube of blood. Quickly the dizziness and weakness kicked in. I was terrified by the results. The "what if I was," was scary, but the "what if I wasn't" was even worse. I felt like I was going to let them down either way. We were tunnel vision and hell-bent on saving Scott, and in these years, that's all we thought about.

What if there is no match? I began to wonder. The drive home was silent. Not because there wasn't much to say, but because I felt like I couldn't speak. I was solely focused on keeping it together, keeping myself "okay" while we waited for the results to come.

The call came in, "Unfortunately, you are not a match" my dad said to me.

I was not a match. I was not a match. I hung up the phone and called Keena. This is what I do when tragedy strikes, I reach to her. I held the phone to my ear and cried to my sister.

"I couldn't even get this one thing right."

"Dash, it's okay. He will find a match, this is not your fault. I love you more than anything okay? You know that right?"

"Yeah, Kee I know. I love you too."

I hang up the phone and wish I could believe her that this isn't on me. But I believe that in some way, my DNA not matching up is my own fault.

It's all your fault Ashleigh, said the voice that I can never escape.

* * *

The bone marrow transplant eventually took place. The medical team was able to create a match and somehow it worked. It came with complications, basically all the complications, but somehow he managed to push through.

During this battle, he can't eat or speak. It takes an even bigger toll on his body than before. The years of treatment are aging him and the small pits under his eyes are turning translucent black. The way I assume they would look during someone's last days. When my dad calls so I can FaceTime him, Scott's lifeless body in the background becomes increasingly disturbing. To be frank, I don't know how my dad looks at it every day. I can barely look at him at all.

Everything in Scott is dying, because this cancer treatment doesn't know how to attack just the bad cells, so they are attacking them all. His body is at war with itself, with the cancer, and with the treatment. And if you could see what he looks like, you would think he is losing and a lot of the time, he is. This is an uphill war, one that we all are praying he will win. Sometimes before I go to sleep, I kiss the picture of him and I on my nightstand, and I beg for him to win.

The cancer still isn't gone and they don't understand why the treatments haven't been enough. He had beaten cancer twice before his twenty-third birthday. But this time, it wouldn't go so easy. Not that it ever did. The doctors led with warnings instead of positivity this time around. The approach is a kill him to save him, mindset. We are nearly out of options. They threw everything at his cancer like a full-on nuclear war. Bombs, bullets, arrows, you name it, they did it. They are out for blood because, obviously, the cancer is too.

"Hey honey, I'm so sorry, but I have bad news. Scott's cancer is resisting the treatments. It's a lot worse this time and we are running out of options" my dad says on the other side of the phone, "we are talking to his team now, but it doesn't look good."

And just like that, I am a root ripped out of the ground. Tears fall from my face just as fast as my body to the floor. He got cancer three times in three years. Cancer that was supposed to be treatable. Cancer that's treatable, just not for him and not for long. We are a little less positive, a little less hopeful, and a lot more worried this time around. In all reality, we have every right to be. There is only one treatment option left.

The third time's the charm, though. Or is it?

Chapter 9: Undocked

I am the first one here, which is not unusual because I am always early. I came back to this house today because Scott is coming also. My dad asked us both to come over so we could spend time together before they both had to leave again. They had a couple of weeks left at home before they had to fly back to Houston to begin another treatment.

I'm sitting on that cream-colored couch in my dad's house as Scott walks in. I look up at him like a kid who just disappointed their parent. I give him the half-smile I often give when I am trying to fake some form of happiness, but I am not good at hiding my expressions and he sees right through it, right through me.

"It's alright" he reminds me with a smile "we'll figure it out."

I stand up quickly to hug him, I wrap my arms around him, noticing that my arms overlap due to his lack of body weight. My arms hit him around the waist because he towers over me. He towers over everyone. Even at five-eight, I still sit almost a foot shorter than him.

Coupled with his height, at least before all of this, he was pretty big. Not as broad as my father, but he was just as strong. When I looked at my scrawny long limbs, it was quite a wonder how I was related to two people who looked straight out of the NFL when I mimicked the body of a praying mantis.

My brother being as big as he was, became the perfect weapon that I often used on people when they tried to mess with me. Everyone close to me has heard me say the infamous "Do I need to call my brother?" phrase. It was the best way to end a tough situation, especially because they knew if I called, he would come, and all hell would break loose. He had that side to him. That natural protector came easy to him, instinctual.

Then, on his other side, he is incredibly tender. You can have one conversation with him and you'll never feel more loved or protected. That's why he is my safety.

When it is time to go into this room, to deal with this pain, my therapist guides me gently. The door is tall and thin, it looks brittle and misshapen. It is the grayish-green color that I love. Just as I grab the matte, gray handle to open the door, she brings up something I never realized before, I count on Scott so much to keep me safe, that I feel exposed and helpless without him. She is right, I walk in to face my truth.

My therapist advised me to un-dock my metaphorical ship from my brother and move it to her. Then, when I am ready, I will dock it to myself. It's all starting to make sense to me. When anything in my life is challenging or scary, I hold on to my brother for dear life because he has always kept me safe. It was a tried-and-true strategy for me, one I wasn't ready to part with. No wonder, when my dock broke because it couldn't protect me anymore, I got completely lost at sea.

That's the problem with codependency, you can't depend on it. You can't depend on someone else to keep you safe, happy, or anything else for that matter. You must depend on yourself, create happiness, and safety for yourself. It's the first hard lesson I had to learn as a young adult, no one can give you those things, they are found inside ourselves. They are just often buried under the crappy things that convinced us otherwise.

If we depend on others for our emotional well-being, even those who are the most dependable, we set ourselves up to lose and we set them up to fail.

In order to find safety, I had to dig down into myself on why I never felt safe in the first place and then I had to deal with it. To feel joy, I had to go to the darkest places in my heart and figure out how to bring some light in. I had to do it, that's the point. The message, no one else could do that for me.

I needed to take care of myself, so I could help my brother through this. So we could all make it through this.

My brother Scott was the only constant thing I had growing up, well he and my stuffed lamb named Lovey. Because while I had loving parents and a slew of four siblings, he was the one I traveled to and from with. My other siblings would go to their dad's house and Scott and I would go to ours.

In the big picture, Scott was the only person who knew both sides of my story, because he was living it alongside me. My brain convinces me that I am only safe if Scott is there. And in some areas of my past, that was my reality, especially when it came to my stepdad and my ex-boyfriend. But, in other moments, it was just my assumption. Maybe I was safe, but I just didn't believe it unless Scott was there.

As I become an adult, I realize that Scott will not be by my side through everything. I am eighteen now, and he has been sick for two years. Scott's health is on the edge, worse than ever before. And here I am, eighteen and clueless. Eighteen and lost. Eighteen and heartbroken. Eighteen and begging for help, but only on the inside. Eighteen, without my brother next to me.

I constantly fight off the thoughts in my head that just kept saying, *if you lose him, you will die too.*

Selfishly, while my brother needed me the most, I am the worst version of myself. Instead of being strong and there for him, instead of becoming his dock, I was just a ship out at sea. I was riding the waves in an empty shell until I started sinking. While my brother fought for his life, I looked for opportunities to fight for mine.

This is when I started throwing myself into chaos. Into unsafe scenarios, drama, and any distraction. Chaos became something I craved. I'd be lying if I said I was sane at the time. I was chasing hurt and it was chasing me. I was young and looking for relief. I was young and I was having a challenging time with everything that was coming up in therapy.

The one thing I do have going for me is that I am finally getting my life together. I am finally seeing the steps I need to take to get closer to healing.

I need to be there for my brother in any capacity that he needs me. So I am on a mission to make sure that I can be. That way, when he comes home on the other side of this, I can be his dock like he always was for me.

I am ready to be there for the brother who made me cereal in the mornings, who braided my hair before school, the brother who I had *Pokémon* wars with and hours-long *Mortal Kombat* challenges. I am ready to help Scott in any way that he will let me. I am prepared to do whatever he needs. It is my turn.

Somehow, this last beautiful and scientifically genius treatment is working. The stem cell transplant would go on to give him the very first cancer-free six-month scan he had gotten since this started. It was clear at one year, two, three, four, and five. It has been clear and stayed clear ever since. He was finally cancer-free. It is over, the war is finally over, and everyone can just breathe, even if only for a moment.

While I can't shut the revolving door of illness, I can shut the one that includes cancer. In fact, I can slam it so hard that the thin door will shatter.

Chapter 10: Wake Me Up When September Ends

When Green Day sang "Wake Me Up When September Ends," they knew what they were talking about. They knew what I had come to learn.

September is the worst month of the year. This is my new understanding. I have been in college for a month now and it's not going great. Scott is only getting worse, as the cancer shrinks from his body. My grades are garbage just like my decision-making. My relationship is only getting more toxic, more unsafe. My self-worth has shrunk to half its size and now this.

Now September of 2012 is here to kick me to what will become my new rock bottom. *As if I could feel any lower than I do right now. As if the universe could lash out at me any harder.*

As I sit here in therapy, I know this is the room I have been avoiding for over a year. This is the one I have convinced myself that I do not need to go in. Duh, I was sad about this. What more was there to understand? Other than the fact that it made me want to give up on my own life, how could there be much to clean up in here?

When I close my eyes, the door is navy blue. It reminds me of water. Like if I open it, the water will uncontrollably flood out and take me with it. I have never felt greater pain than when my brother died. I don't want to relive this. But, I have to. I open the door and hold my breath as the waves burst out and tackle me in grief.

This type of emotional suffering somehow hurts even physically. Opening the door invites in so much pain. My entire chest tightens, I feel like I cannot breathe, everything else goes numb and my throat hurts, like there's a scream about to literally rip through it. This is the end of my life, as I know it and I am not ready to relive it.

I place my hands on my knees and inhale as big of a breath as I can. One, because I feel like I can't breathe, and two to buy myself some time. I don't want to go into this room again, which is why I must. The metaphorical door remains just as it was before. Except this time, the water is leaking out from underneath. It is yearning to get out. It is leaking all over me. I just know that when I open it again, I am going to get lost in it. But, my therapist is here and I know she will guide me through it. I take a step in and I immediately see it.

Purple, silk sheets.

I was sound asleep covered in those sheets in that old, beat-up apartment. I didn't have class until later that day, so I was taking in the complete luxury of sleeping in. That was the luxury that college offered, you didn't have to schedule morning classes if you didn't want to, and I didn't. The gift I gave myself was no classes before nine am. I was in a deep sleep, one that allowed me to miss over a dozen missed calls. The dream I was lost in was quickly interrupted as I felt someone grab my arms and begin to shake me. The grip was tight and the shaking was panicked. It was the kind of sensation that woke your body up in terror because you knew something was incredibly wrong. I immediately tensed up, almost frozen. I sat myself up in bed to help fully wake up, I did this to ensure I could see what was going on. I made sure I did this slowly. I was dreading whatever was coming and I wasn't in a rush to figure out what it was. *What did I do now?* I assumed in my head.

Cody only woke me up like this when he was mad at me. The shaking was increasing in intensity, not only was he shaking me, but I could feel that he was shaking himself. I must have seriously screwed up this time. I knew it by the look in his light eyes when I finally, hesitantly opened mine. I couldn't put off waking up any longer, my avoidance was becoming evident. Under his shaggy dark hair, I could see that his eyes were soaked, his face red and splotchy. Whatever it was, it was bad enough that he was crying.

The words came out in slow motion, "Your mom has been trying to get a hold of you all morning Ash. She called me at work, your brother...he died, they found him this morning" he shakily sputtered out.

It felt too big for him, I felt sorry for him having to be the one to tell me this. Neither one of us would ever be able to forget this moment.

I would spend years trying to bury it. As I go back to this memory now, eleven years later, my core still tightens, my throat buckles and the tears flood me. This time, I let them. But at that moment, I did not. I was full of confusion and rage. The first image that came to mind was that my siblings and I would no longer be the five that we once knew, but that image of just us four was too much to handle, so I shoved it down hard. *If one goes, we all go.*

I buried the thought and began to sputter out questions.

"I thought the chemo was working, did something go

wrong? Was it something with the transplant? Was it too muc-"

Just to be interrupted with, "It wasn't Scott, Ash. It was Ryan."

What?

"What do you mean? That doesn't make any sense. Ryan's fine."

I just assumed it was Scott because of his illness, because he was so sick. The lesson this day taught me, was that you can lose anyone, any time, any day, and there is nothing more important than loving the people around you while you still have the chance because you truly never know when you'll run out of time.

We were out of time.

I am out of time.

* * *

The pain of remembering this moment is too much, so I divert my focus to memories of Ryan, many of which ironically include almost losing him due to his daredevil nature in the first place. As a kid, I looked up to my brother Ryan as a caregiver, because he so often was that for me. My mom worked multiple jobs to make ends meet, and raising five kids as a single mother was no easy task. As the last of five, I was babied by the others.

While my mother works, Ryan being the oldest, is left in charge. But, for the sake of being honest, Keena, my oldest sister, who was number two, was truly the one in charge, it was our unspoken system. Because Ryan was usually too busy beating one of us at some video game to watch us all. He had some talent in this area.

When I close my eyes to picture Ryan, because that is how I can picture him best, his smile takes up his entire face. It's the type of smile he only gave when he was with his son or when he was fishing, but in my mind, I get to pretend like he is smiling just for me. I can see his deep brown hair sticking up all crazy like it often was due to his unnatural amount of cowlicks. I can picture his almond-shaped hazel eyes looking right back at me and his broad frame reaching out for one of his painfully tight-squeezing brother bear hugs. I can picture him as who he was at his best. With a huge fish in his hands and a goofy expression on his face.

Sometimes, when I picture him, I am taken back to a memory that horrified me as a kid. I was lying in bed with my mother when we heard a faint knock on the door. The sun had just come up to remind us that it was morning. My mom grabbed her red silk robe and tied it around herself as she walked down the hall to open the door. I decided I should tip-toe behind her to see who was there. I peeked around the wall and saw my big brother's broad frame collapse into her as soon as she opened the front door. He was much taller than her, but not as big as

Scott. Ryan stood a little closer to six-two and had a stockier frame. Even so, my strong mother could hold him up.

His hair was wet with blood, and so was his face, his clothes, his entire body. She began to panic, and rattled out "We have to go to the hospital!" "What happened to you?" she said in a tone like she was half worried sick and half pissed off at him for putting himself in this position.

"I'm good. I need some sleep and I'll be fine" my brother responded so cavalierly.

My mom looked at him like he was nuts and forced him into her minivan. She grabbed me next, "It's going to be okay" she whispered to me as she buckled my car seat.

The drive from our house to the hospital was about fifteen minutes and fifteen of those minutes were spent with me trying to avoid all eye contact with my brother.

I kept telling myself "Don't look, don't look, don't look."

If I didn't see it, it wouldn't feel so scary. Plus, it was pretty gross and I felt like at any moment I was going to throw up and make matters worse. I could only protect myself from the scene, but not the sounds. The sound of my brother gasping for air made me more nervous and more uncomfortable with every minute that passed.

The silver minivan whipped into the emergency room parking lot and immediately doctors and nurses came running out with a gurney. My mom had given them a heads-up on the mess we were bringing in. They immediately opened the van door and dragged his body out of it. I watched as they placed him on the gurney and just as I looked up, the doctor lifted his arm and slammed a tube into my brother's chest. I managed to keep the vomit in my mouth as it came up.

My tiny hand wrapped around my mouth as I begged myself to swallow it and my other hand reached up to wipe the massive tears that began to convulse out of me.

I tried to stay focused on my brother as they ran him into the hospital while my mom found a spot to park the van. I unbuckled myself and jumped out quickly as we needed to follow them closely behind. The hospital employees let us know where to go and I took my mom's hand as she pulled me with her up to the ICU. When we got there, she took some time to call the rest of the family. While she called, I stared through the glass window at my brother in the hospital bed.

"I'm sorry I wouldn't look at you" I whispered to the glass.

We spent the entire day there, rotating between Ryan's room and the waiting room, trying to give everyone a chance to see him, with a family as big as ours it can take a while. There were some jokes made about him having nine lives in the waiting room as an attempt to lighten the mood. It was true, he flirted with danger more times than most.

"He has a collapsed lung, some broken bones, and bruises, but overall, we expect him to make a full recovery. It will take some time though and he will be in the ICU for a few more days" I overheard the doctor tell my mother as he walked her back to Ryan's room.

I would wait for her to come back and tell the others. Mostly because I didn't really understand what any of it meant. I just barely understood that the reason I had to see him slam a tube into my brother's chest was because he couldn't breathe. That explained the noises I heard on the way over. Only my brother could survive a car accident like that. The truck rolled and he was in the bed of it. It threw him from the vehicle and it rolled on top of him. We were lucky he was still alive at all.

My youngest in the family dynamic started to change little by little in these moments. I started to learn from my siblings simply by watching them. What I learned the most was how to bounce back after a tragedy. How to be strong like Ryan, Keena, Kendra, and Scott. How to be strong just like my siblings.

* * *

In therapy, it was finally time to enter the parts of this room that I had been avoiding. I had unpacked some of it, methodically avoiding the parts that I felt I didn't need to understand or clean up. It was the pairing of the two hard admissions: the loss and the aftermath. My brother died, and I knew why I was sad. There wasn't much to learn or unpack here. But what I was hiding from wasn't his death. It was who I became afterward. That's what really scared me.

Once we got through a childhood memory that was easier to talk about, it was time to go into the parts of the room that I really needed to see. To September 28th, 2012. The date that would be marked by my family as the worst day of our lives for years to come. I hate September 28th.

I close my eyes to tune into this room again. My therapist is with me.

We spend a lot of time worrying about the things that we understand, but what about the things that we don't? I didn't understand how I could have one brother fighting for his life while my other brother lost his. I couldn't fathom any of this being my reality, but at just eighteen years old, it was.

The assumptions began pouring into my head like toxic poison. Did he drink himself to death . . . did he do this on purpose . . . did he . . . did he . . . was it my fault? Was there something we could have done? We should have seen this coming. We should have been more worried. We should have been there and we weren't. We knew he was struggling, we knew he had been drinking too much. The guilt became all-consuming. We failed him, I thought. I failed him.

The shock hit me first, then the guilt, then the grief. But grief wouldn't come for a while. I was too angry. My body and my brain denied everything for as long as they could. It immediately shut down my emotions. It made me cold, hard, and stoic. I had to be strong. I convinced myself that being strong meant feeling nothing so that I could survive this. All I felt was numb and painful confusion. And then I found out it wasn't the drinking. It was an accident. I felt even worse because of my assumptions.

In the minutes after the news, I called my father. He was still in Houston at M.D. Anderson with Scott because this all happened during one of his treatments. Something inside me begged to hear his voice. I needed him to tell me that Scott was okay. I needed to know that I still had a brother left. I needed rock-solid proof. I was desperate for something to hold on to.

As if anything would make a difference. Either way, a part of me would die today and I would never get it back. The five was now four.

I spent the rest of the day worrying about Scott and my sisters, Keena and Kendra. I would call them all up individually. I needed to make sure that everyone was okay, even though I knew that they weren't.

I worried about my mother. About anyone and everyone else, but me. I couldn't imagine how Scott felt, hearing about our brother passing when he was in the middle of his own fight for his life. How could he have the strength to fight both battles at the same time?

I worried about my sister, Keena. I knew she would take on so much worry that never belonged to her. She revolves her entire life around taking care of us all, I worried she would forget to take care of herself. I could visually picture her large, brown eyes, full of pain and willpower to do anything to protect her family. That's just how she operates, we wouldn't have gotten through much without her.

I worried about Kendra, that she would feel alone, that she would be on a ship without her dock. A fear I so often feared for myself had just become her reality. I worried about her because she was not the type to ask for help, but in her gray-blue eyes, I could always tell when she needed it. I hoped that she would lean on me.

And then finally, I worried about myself and it scared me. Because I felt like I couldn't live through this. I felt this terrifying feeling that this would kill me too.

Then, it came to me. My mom. My mom who was already watching one child suffer, just lost her oldest son and there was nothing in the world that I can imagine that would be worse than that. So, I called her as I drove to school. Her voice broke my heart. It shook with pain as she immediately began apologizing to me.

"I didn't want you to find out like this. I wanted to tell you. It's already on Facebook and I had to make sure someone told you before you got on and saw it."

I was disgusted, random people had already posted it on Facebook before all the family had been notified. People waste no time.

I interrupted her and let her know, "I have to go to class. I will be home after."

"But Ashleigh," she responded.

"I can't miss another day, Mom" I callously replied.

It was heartless of me, but I couldn't talk to her. It was too painful.

My body knew survival mode well. It knew how to shut down everything, it knew how to go numb, how to block out, to disassociate. It knew that in order to survive, feelings could wait.

I was only allowed to miss four days of my college Spanish class or it was an automatic fail. I had already missed three, so regardless of what just happened, I went. I walked in feeling cold. Looked around shocked at the pure emptiness a full room could bring. I quickly found an empty desk and took my place, I didn't have friends here, I just needed to be a body in a room so I could pass. Ten minutes went by, and I felt myself slowly losing my grip. Every inch of emotion and hurt that I had buried, shoved, and locked down was forcefully beginning to burst out.

I quickly wiped the tears as they came, hoping to hide them before they fell. The nausea began to erupt, I was sick with grief. I went up to my professor's desk, with all my things in hand, and quietly told him my situation through my pouring down tears. He looked up at me like I had said something stupid. Like I just gave him a "dog ate my homework" excuse.

"Well, if you bring me a death certificate, I can excuse you. Many students make things like this up with their grandparents, so that is my rule now" he stated in a matter-of-fact kind of way.

But this wasn't a matter-of-fact kind of moment. It was a matter of humanity, my brother just died and my professor's response was "I need proof."

It took everything in me not to flip him off as I walked out the door. I ran out of that classroom and let the door slam behind me. Every step I ran down on that cream-colored staircase felt like a mile. All I could do was run. I sobbed, and I ran to my car in hopes of out-running this feeling. I knew I would never come back here, not after that.

When I got home, there were so many cars outside. I couldn't bring myself to go in. To face them. To face my mother. I sat in that car, and I let all that pain pour out of me. It came out in screams. In punches to the steering wheel. In tight grips around my leather car seats and tears so big that it hurt as they came out. This grief would take me with it.

Shock is an incredibly powerful thing, but it was fading and reality was sinking in more with every breath. It felt like a knife, that slowly, but forcefully was being shoved straight into my heart. It physically was so painful, like a piece of me was being ripped out and shredded right in front of me. I had to force myself to think of anyone else, but myself. The more I thought about myself and my pain, the more it pulled me under.

I began to worry about my nephew, how would a five-year-old boy ever begin to understand the loss of his father? And would he even remember who he was when he grew up?

The worry began to spread. It grew over me in a monstrous way that felt like an uphill battle I was bound to lose. I had to stop. I had to stop thinking and find something I could control. Then it came to me, I am the "therapist of the family." That is what everyone says. So, it will be my job to help everyone through this. That's what I can do. I can help. Or so I thought.

In the weeks following, that is exactly what I would do. I would answer every call of a crying family member and I would talk to them about everything they were feeling. I would offer the best advice an eighteen-year-old could think of, but more importantly, I would just listen. I would listen, I would understand, and I would love.

I did it to myself. I worried that if I couldn't carry my now three siblings through this, we would never make it out. The pressure began to weigh heavily like bricks on my chest. No one made it my job, I just always felt like it was. I was the peace-keeper, the one who wanted to keep everyone safe, the one everyone would come to. I wondered how I could help them through this, how I was going to help my mom through this. I didn't know how to help because I didn't think I was ever going to get through this.

If there is one thing grief has taught me, it is that it comes in waves. Some of these waves you can ride out, cry when you need to, and rest when you can. Some waves are so small that just for tiny moments you can pretend that they aren't there. Like those tears in your eyes that no one sees because they're just small enough that they never come down. Then, there are waves that are massive. They are all-consuming. They are dark, sightless, and they feel like drowning. They rise over your head and pull you under with every ounce of their unbearable weight.

In the years that followed Ryan's death, the waves were constantly this way. They never took a break and I had to fight every second to prevent myself from drowning.

When my family set up a date and time to go see Ryan's body and say goodbye, I agreed that I wanted to go.

My mom made sure not to pressure us with this, she told us, "It is your choice how you wish to remember him, it is up to you if you want to see him or not."

Even though she kept reminding us of this, I felt like I had to go. Like what kind of sister would I be if I do not go say goodbye to him at the mortuary? That pressure I put on myself only made my anxiety so much worse. I had no clue what to expect, but the images my imagination kept creating terrified me and it felt like I was awaiting the scariest moment of my life.

The day was here and I faintly heard the car engine as my mother and my sister Keena pulled in to pick me up. It would just be the three of us.

Scott was unable to come as he was still in Texas in the middle of a horrendous treatment. No matter how hard they tried, he was not stable enough to travel, not even for this.

Kendra decided that for her, she wanted her last memory of him to be the one she already had. It was a good one and she didn't want to trade her last time seeing her brother for one as grim as this. I started to think that she was right about this decision. And, I was grateful that she made this choice an option for me too.

It is hard to know what the right thing to do in these moments is. So in the car, my mother and my sister Keena waited for me. I stood up to walk out the door to meet them and the second I took the first step out of the house and immediately started throwing up in the grass.

My sister Keena jumped out and put an arm around me. "It's okay Dash. You don't have to come okay? It's okay, he would understand" she said as she rubbed my back.

"Girls, I'm sorry, but we have to get going," my mom said through the car window.

I wiped the vomit from my mouth with my sleeve and looked up to give her a defeated smile. I would not be joining them.

"I'm sorry I cannot look at you" I cried into the dirt.

Chapter 11: Saying Goodbye

While I believe that grief, with time, does become more bearable, I do not feel like it is a room that you can ever fully leave. Grief is not a permanent state of being, but it is a permanent feeling that while it may shrink, never goes away entirely. At least, not for me.

As I sit here in therapy, I am frustrated as I realize this.

"I have been coming to you for about a year, so I guess I'm just wondering how long it takes until I get better?" I ask my therapist.

"What do you mean by 'get better?'" She responds.

"Like, when will I not be sad anymore? I know I am changing a lot and I am really proud of that, but I still feel like I am just as sad. I want to know how long I need to come until I don't feel like crap anymore?"

"There is no cure, Ashleigh. Things can definitely get better, but none of these things will ever completely go away," she reminds me.

I know she is right, but I can't help but feel disappointed. I want to feel better. I want this to go away.

The answer she gave me feels so obvious now. My brother died. Of course, I am always going to be sad. But I was dying not to feel sad anymore, not to feel anything. The only thing scarier than losing him was how frequently I thought the words, *I don't want to be here anymore.* It scared me how frequently I thought about giving up. How sometimes it sounded better than fighting through it. It sounded easier, but deep down, I know that it isn't.

The only way I was going to find peace, was when I made it through the pain. I reached for the blue door again and let the waves take me back to the days that followed the death of my brother.

A few months before Ryan passed, I had a weekend trip planned to go visit my brother Scott in Houston. I hadn't seen him since he left town for his treatments, it had been a few months already and I missed him and my father so much. Ryan just passed away during the same week in which I am supposed to leave for my visit. September 28 was a Friday, and my flight was scheduled to leave on Monday.

My mom insisted that I didn't cancel my trip.

"Ash, it will be good for you to go. The funeral will take a few days to plan and it might be best if you aren't home for it all" she said to me, just as she pulled me in for one of her pain-curing hugs.

I instantly feel lighter. As she holds me, she whispers "Scotty probably needs you right now. You should go."

Once she brings up Scott, there is no turning back. I am going.

I rush in to pack my things, just comfortable outfits because I know we are going to be in the hospital ninety-nine percent of the time, but my dad told me to throw in a couple of nice outfits for dinners. He has some plans of his own to try and bring a little joy into our hearts, the way that good food often can.

I get on the flight in the only airport our small town has to offer. I wait anxiously to see my father and my brother. I am so excited to see them, but so nervous at the same time. My dad has warned me that Scott does not look well, but nothing could have prepared me for just how bad it was.

When I landed, I traded one heartbreak for another. Instead of focusing on the loss of my brother that I was still refusing to face, I was forced to focus on my other brother in the hospital bed before me.

He doesn't even look like himself anymore. He is barely alive and not healthy enough to even notice my arrival. I walk into the room slowly, and he just barely turns his head to acknowledge me. His swollen eyes are barely open, just enough to reveal the deep brown color that they are. Even a task as minute as lifting his eyelids looks difficult for him. His mouth hangs slightly open and he has chemo sores all around his face. As I look closely, I can see that his tongue is missing a chunk of it. It looks like it has been cut in half. The chemo is literally eating away at him from the inside out. His fingernails are yellow, dead, and falling off. His body is weightless, skinnier than I had ever seen him, while his face remains so puffy and swollen. And his bald head, which shows every vein because of his translucent skin.

He looks dead or very close to it. I assume this has to be the closest one could be to death while still alive. It is horrifying. The harsh reality that I came to at this moment was, I might lose both of my brothers. How was I supposed to live through that? I feel so small knowing that when I fly home for the funeral, Scott won't be joining me. Neither would my father. They couldn't. I would return alone. It is heartbreaking, but it is obvious, he can barely open his eyes and sit up in bed. There is no way either of them could come. Not only is he barely alive himself, but he isn't going to get closure at our brother's funeral either. He would miss this moment like he was forced to miss so many others. I never thought I would feel grateful to go to a funeral, until now.

The entire trip, each day was the same. My dad had been doing this for six-month periods at a time for the last two years. As we walk into the condo, I am pleasantly surprised by how at home I feel. My father rented this place in Houston so that he and Scott would have a place to stay during treatments. It was better than a hotel because it offered privacy and a lot less people. Which in turn means less exposure to germs for my brother. I am glad that my father found the condo at least it can offer the two of them a place to give them a "home-like" feel. It allows them to have their own rooms when Scott is able to leave the hospital and it allows for family members to come stay without having to worry about finding a hotel nearby.

The condo is mostly occupied by my father, though, as Scott spends most of his time in a hospital bed. I walked to the guest room and decide to turn in, the place came fully furnished and it reminded me of something people would rent out while they were on vacation. For a second while I lay here, I try to pretend that I am. I know we have a long weekend ahead of us.

Morning comes early, and we grab to-go food to ensure we arrive at the hospital bright and early. As we walk in, we both grab a seat and sit there quietly. We have masks on our faces, yellow gowns on our bodies that cover our clothes, and blue gloves on our hands. And as we sit here, I find it easy to hide my true emotions behind this hospital gear.

We sit quietly and exchange a few whispers because Scott cannot really speak, and we can never actually tell if he is awake or not. We did this until it was time for lunch. Then, we would go eat, come back to the hospital, leave again for dinner, then go back one last time to see Scott until it was time to head home to get ready for bed. Eat. Sleep. Stare at my brother in pain. That was what we did. That's what my father has been doing for years. It is numbing.

Don't get me wrong, there is nowhere else I would rather be. But I couldn't help but notice the toll it was taking on my father. He looks less like himself the more that time goes on. His once tan golfer skin is now gray and lacking in color. His hazel eyes look dull and red. His tall and broad frame is now slender, but he doesn't look healthy. He had lost a ton of weight, muscle included, and I am anxious that he is neglecting himself as he takes on this role as the caretaker.

It is a daunting task to spend your time watching the person you love suffer all day long, every day for months and years. I can't seem to fathom how my father is doing it. All while somehow remaining positive and strong. Even though he was beginning to look restless and weak.

"Dad, I'm worried."

"Honey, I know. We all are."

"No, Dad. I am worried about you."

"Me? I'm fine" he says as he grabs the waist of his pants and shimmies them up. The way he does when he cracks a joke or says something silly about himself.

"You don't look fine, Dad. You look like you're going to have a heart attack. We need you to be healthy. You need to take care of yourself too."

"I know, honey. I'm fine," he said.

He would never admit how hard this all was on him. I think we all feel selfish admitting it is hard on us as we watch how much Scott is suffering. Our problems seem so insignificant compared to his. They seem so small.

It doesn't help that Scott fights so gracefully. He is relentless and inspiring. He refuses to break down, to tell anyone besides family much about it, and he never once showed weakness. I find myself grieving him daily, even though he is still here with us, it feels like he is so far away. Yet, here he is, never complaining, just fighting through. If he doesn't show his hand, I feel like I can't show mine either. I keep my suffering to myself.

Tonight is my second night here, I can't bring myself to sleep. I toss and turn under these teal blankets, but I just keep seeing both of my brothers' faces and I can't shake my fears or my feelings.

I know that when I get back home, I will have to face the other half of my grief. I will have to stand up in front of our family and our friends and give a speech. Watching Scott, I know this is a luxury, but it still feels like an awful chore, that I want to do, but am scared to do. It is hard to not let my mind think about the very real possibility that I might have to write two of these speeches at an incredibly young age. *I wonder what I would say*. The second the thought escaped me, I shut it down. Nope, Scott's going to pull through. That cannot happen to my family.

I sit up in bed and begin writing my speech for Ryan's funeral. I know I want to speak, but I don't know what to say. How could a speech written by an eighteen-year-old girl ever be worthy enough for Ryan's funeral? I have a million memories of him growing up, but so little with him as an adult, I had just barely become one, if you could call me that. I wasn't really acting like one. I feel too small for this task. So, instead of trying to sound a certain way, I open my heart and let it pour onto the page. I grabbed a pen off the nightstand, sat in bed with my knees up for a table, and opened my black journal to the first blank page. The pen started moving before my thoughts were clear, my heart knew what it needed to say.

* * *

They say God gives his worst battles to his strongest soldiers. If that's true, he must think my family is invincible. While we gather here, we are missing two important men in our lives. My brother Scott, who couldn't be here with us today. And my brother Ryan, who will never be with us, at least in this form, again. Ryan was the big brother that every girl needs. His bear hugs could literally wash away hurt, away pain. Growing up with him was never dull or boring. He was the life of the party in any situation and his loud voice easily filled every room. He was an incredible person, a protective brother, and an amazing father. One of our favorite memories was when I was super young, and he would babysit all four of us while my mother had to work nights. He made sure to follow my mom's rules, something he often did not do and refused to let me eat my goldfish in the living room. This led to a few phone calls to the police department from my four-year-old self because this seemed so mean that it just had to be illegal, I knew it. I quickly learned that this was not a legal matter, but it seemed like it should be to me. This memory always warms my heart, just like all the others of him watching me. I can still hear him calling me "chicken" and I will always remember his laugh. But the most important memory he left me with was the love that he made me feel. I will miss you forever, Ryan. Life will never be the same. I love you.

If only they taught us how to write a funeral speech in school, my brain mocked. No matter what I wrote, it never felt like it would ever be worthy. How do you sum up life? A sibling? The five of us were each other's whole worlds and now one-fifth of our world is gone. We are incomplete. In our hearts. In our souls.

I couldn't keep my mind from slipping into the darkness, I couldn't help but wonder if I would have to write two funeral speeches for both of my brothers before I was old enough to even walk into a bar. I was reminded that *you can't think this way*, but it was hard not to. It was hard to deny the worst-case scenario, even though I begged God to never let it come to fruition.

I also begged for clarity. There is nothing quite like a loss when it comes to examining life. How fragile it is, how short it can be. How easily it can end, and what you want to leave behind when it does. When my brother died, I became uncomfortably aware that someday my life would also end, and in this realization, I knew that I had to stop taking mine for granted.

I needed to leave my boyfriend and I promised myself I would as soon as I got back to town. I wasn't going to show up to my brother's funeral with him. I wasn't going to disappoint Ryan one more time.

I also knew that I needed to figure out what I wanted out of life and what that required of me. But, before I could even go there, before I could even try, I would have to first get lost in my grief. So, I did. I got lost and I shut the door.

Chapter 12:
Getting Familiar with Grief

As I sit here in therapy, I know that we have unfinished business to attend to. Our hour time limit that we both agreed to honor saved me from having to stay in the room that hurt the most, for too long. I managed to get through the basics, the key details of September 28, and the days that followed. Those were by far some of the worst days of my life, but truthfully, the day you pray will bring closure hurts even more. Something about a funeral, a goodbye, a burial site. Those things crawled beneath my skin and haunted me more. I opened that blue door just to be swallowed up again.

I drove myself to the funeral. As I pulled into the first spot I could find in the church parking lot, I had to do a double-take to confirm that she was really in front of me. My lifelong friend, the one I met when I was two in daycare, the one that sat on my hamster and accidentally killed it, the one whose birthday candles I always blew out, the one that couldn't kill the fish, Leah. She is leaning against the hood of her car with her big brown worried eyes and arms wide open.

"I didn't know you were coming," I burst into tears and fell into her arms.

"I started driving the second I heard. I would never miss this" she replied.

She moved to Utah for college, and I hadn't seen her since summer. This was not the reunion we anticipated, but it felt like a huge relief to have her here for me. I needed her more than she knew, more than I would admit.

We walked into the church together and I hugged her goodbye as I approached the aisle doors, only to be greeted by my other best friend, Kenzi. I knew she would be here. I'm still so grateful to her mother for forcing her to become my friend in the seventh grade. She would become such an essential part of my life. I hugged her and thanked her for coming. It was time for me to go where I was dreading, inside the church.

My brother's friend walked me down to my family, where I joined my sisters, my nephew's mother, and my mom.

My nephew, being only five, could not quite handle the gravity of the funeral. He came in for a minute, but he quickly became overwhelmed and upset. I watched as his tiny frame quickly hurried out. He moved so fast that his blue superhero cape with the "R" in the middle flew up as he passed. It looked like he was actually flying. His mother had someone take him to a separate room until the service was over. It's all too much for someone so small. It was too much for me.

With each step down the aisle, I felt repulsed. I felt like I could barely move my feet like I was walking through water, the way it feels when you try to run in a dream. The resistance to reality was unbecoming. I refused to let it sink in.

I looked around and tried to take it all in. The vases of flowers were everywhere. The color blue laced throughout, even more heavily in the crowd. So many people here showed up in his favorite color. I would never wear that blue blazer or those blue pumps again.

And then, I saw the one image I was avoiding, the one so hard to avoid as it was in the center of the stage, right in front of me, so close to me, my brother in a coffin. I tried not to look at it and I tried even harder not to think about him being inside.

It became increasingly hard for me to be in that church, knowing that he was. He felt so far away, yet he was only a few feet away from me. I was eager to get out of there. It felt like if I didn't leave soon, it would take me too.

Voice after voice echoed into the microphone, telling us how great he was, how much he would be missed. He already was. My brother Scott wrote an incredible speech from his hospital bed, one which he had a family friend read. One that he would not be able to. I suddenly felt guilty for being so nervous to read mine. *At least I can*, I thought. Everything my brother missed brought me so much sadness, but it also taught me to not take anything for granted, not even the smallest of things.

As the speeches came to a close, it was our turn. The three of us sisters would get up and one by one we would brave the mic.

My oldest sister Keena spoke first. Even though she was the oldest sister, she stood the shortest. Her rich chocolate brown hair was full of volume, and it hung just to the middle of her back. I watched as her shaky, yet confident hand took the mic, she glanced at us with a "it's going to be okay" smile and then she began. Her courage carried her through, but she didn't have it for selfish reasons, she had it because she was the oldest sister and she wanted to show us we could do it too. That we were all strong enough. She was so good at setting examples for us all.

Kendra's turn came next. Kendra is very similar to me in that she feels like she can hardly stand up here at all. She stands roughly the same height as me, both of us a solid two inches above Keena. Kendra's blonde hair brings light around her red face and neck. She always turns red and splotchy like this when she's upset. Her blue eyes are bright, the way they get when she cries, and I hear her cloudy voice pour out of her.

As she talks, I take deep breaths as I know my turn is coming. I held my sisters' hands as we each took turns. We stood so closely together up there that there was not even an inch between us. We were leaning on each other in even a literal form.

I can't remember one thing either of them said. I was too focused on what I wanted to say. I don't have all the memories from this day, they're blotchy, but I do remember the way it felt for us girls to stand up there without our brothers and the emptiness we felt without them.

I remember the way their words grabbed my heart, brought me comfort, and shattered me all at the same time. I remember thinking that just us three felt like hell and all I wanted was for us to be the five again.

I was proud of myself that I was able to read my speech. It is not a skill set I normally have, but a certain and unexpected strength grabbed ahold of me up there as I spoke. I like to think that it was my brother, somehow his infectious energy remained.

I like to remember that in this moment, I did something that I never thought I could do. I hid behind my long dark hair and read from my paper. And when I finished, the quote came to me, the quote I would get tattooed on my body the next day. I finally understood it. I don't remember where I first heard it, but I knew it to be true. *You never know how strong you are, until being strong is the only choice you have.* That is a fact, I just survived, my definition of the un-survivable. Barely, but here I am.

The church is massive and full of so many faces of people whose lives he touched. Just for a moment, looking into that crowd, I felt something unexpected, I felt joy. His life was short, but it had so much meaning.

My sisters and I walked back to take our seats and we sat down next to my mother. My mother, who would not give a speech, who could not speak, who could barely sit, barely breathe, barely be there at all. My mother who in the coming weeks, would evaporate into her grief entirely.

My mother was not quick to leave. Unlike the rest of us, who were struggling to be in here any longer. She was struggling to walk away. She was treating this moment like her last goodbye, the last time she would be this close to her son. But we were nearing the end.

The speeches are over, the preacher has spoken, the prayers have been said. The slideshow and the music nearing an end, thank God. It was intensely painful to watch these images of my family, my brother, his son, and his friends pass by knowing that he would never be in another picture again. His thick, dark hair was crazy in almost all of them, his outdated white sunglasses sitting on top of it all. His hazel eyes were full of life, and his smile was massive in each one. Every other picture included my nephew or a fish. The two things that brought him the most happiness. His son and fishing.

And while the images rotate, Diamond Rio's song "One More Day" is playing in the background. I never want to hear that song again. Even a decade later, it would still make me sick. I didn't get one more second, let alone a day.

The slideshow closed us out, it was time to say goodbye, and my mother was not ready. We would never be ready. Each one of us took turns walking up to the coffin, all of us doing the same thing. Placing a delicate hand on it, whispering "I love you" as we walked away. Followed by a *screw this*, at least from me.

My mother would not follow our lead, she would not place a delicate hand. There was nothing delicate about this, it was so damn heavy. She walked up slowly, wiping her tears, but she could never wipe them fast enough, they would never stop falling. She draped herself over his coffin, an attempt at one last hug goodbye. I turned back around and watched as she held on for her own life. This image has a permanent slot in the saddest parts of my mind.

This image can bring me to my knees at any moment. I have no control over the grief this memory makes me feel.

I can picture it perfectly, even though my head has begged me to forget. As kids, our parents are these insanely strong hero-like beings. So, when we start to see them as struggling humans, just like us, we realize how fragile we truly are. As I watched, I noticed her legs buckling underneath her, and I immediately went to help lift her up and force her out. "We have to leave Mom, come on" I said, as I struggled to get us both out of there.

Every step I took walking out of that funeral felt like a mile, the aisle went on forever. I stared at my royal blue pumps, his favorite color, and watched each step that I took, slowly, but carefully trying to escape.

I tried to focus on anything other than reality. There were so many people. It felt like a show. So many people wanted to talk to us, hug us, and extend their sympathies, but I just couldn't hear any of it. My anger was so loud. My whole body was too full, about to burst and I just couldn't fit another thing inside my head. I was ripping at the seams. What came out as "thank you" was truly just a bunch of cuss words that I wanted to scream.

After the funeral, I went home to my father's house. I ran down the stairs to my bedroom in the basement. I let my body collapse to the floor without even trying to catch myself on the way down. There was no point anymore, nothing could hurt worse than this. I crawl my limp body through my bedroom and into my bathroom. I pull myself up by the counter and I don't recognize the girl in the mirror. I don't know who I am anymore. I step into my shower, turn on the water, and melt to the bottom. I lay down and for what feels like forever, I watch as the water splashes off my shoes. I cry into that stone floor until the tears run out. I hug myself tightly because it is getting harder to hang on. And then I start to pray. To beg that the water will wash away the pain, that it will wash away me.

* * *

A few months go by, and I begin to shut down little by little. I feel like Alice, except there is no Wonderland. There is just darkness as I fall down into this hole. Further and further. I lose my sense of direction, of hope, of care. I dropped out of college and let go of all my dreams that are attached to it. They all seemed so insignificant now. It all does. Life does. I let the waves of grief take me, and I float out into the abyss without a single care of what will happen to me. It's hard to save someone once they have already drowned.

As I sit here in therapy, an entire year later. I realize I must come to terms with some things, and it is anything, but simple or easy. The facts are, I am never going to hear my big brother's voice again. So, my beloved nicknames like "Chicken" regarding my legs and "Fat Head" regarding my ego, would be put to rest with him. I wasn't that full of myself growing up, but I pretended to be to survive the sibling bullying that comes with being the youngest of five. OK, maybe I was full of myself, but I still thought he was wrong. No way could my fat head sink the Titanic. I didn't care what Ryan said, there was no way that was true.

I was never going to feel my brother's big bear hugs again. His seat would always be empty at Christmas, Easter, Thanksgiving, and birthdays to come. He wasn't going to be at my wedding. He would never get to meet my future husband. Or even worse, my daughters, his nieces. He wasn't going to see his own son grow up, not in the human sense at least. He was going to miss it all. And I had to find a way to be okay with that.

A big part of me felt like we shouldn't move on or be happy without him, that's why for so long, I didn't. I turned my life upside down after he passed, in all the wrong ways. I made sure the only things he missed were things he would never be proud of. Like quitting school and giving up on everything that came after. Ryan was gone. Scott could barely live his life at all, so why should I get to live mine?

I couldn't accept it. I couldn't imagine that these wounds would ever stop hurting me. The harshest reality of all is that they didn't. It's been over ten years now and still on some days the pain wins and completely takes me. There isn't a single beautiful moment in my life that is not painted with a hint of sadness due to him not being a part of it.

What I have learned to accept is that grief does not always stay all-consuming. What once was a massive block in my head, is now something that orbits. With time, healing, and a whole lot of tears I have learned that grief never goes away, but it does get better.

Sometimes that orbit is in the back of your head, and you can just be incredibly happy. Sometimes it's on the side, where the pain is there, but the good is too. And sometimes that damn orbit is smack in the middle of your face. Then, it's time to cry it out man, and let those tears fall. It's time to feel all that you feel. To talk, to ask for help, to eat the peanut butter out of the jar. Whatever it takes, you do it. Those days where it is in your face are the days you never forget. Their birthdays, the holidays, and the day they left this Earth. But, sometimes, when I let myself lean in, I can feel him on those days too.

Ryan is a door I can never close because he is always with me. This door would be left cracked open.

I guess if you're looking for someone to tell you that there are strategies to make the hurt stop for good, I am not your girl. I asked my therapist that question more times than I can count. I tried everything.

But when will I be better? When will I not be sad anymore? How many visits will it take?

The answer is a lifetime. There is no cure for grief. The pains that come from life are too complex. It is not something that can be erased and that is exactly why it is worth living.

Things get better, sure, but they never go away. It takes a lot of time and a lot of work to muddle through our issues to get to a place where we can be happy, but it is so worth it. In order to become everything we want, to chase the life of our dreams, we have to accept that even when "we have it all figured out" the grief will still be there. Grief can bring you to your knees, but sometimes that is the best place to gain perspective. Grief is a solid teacher. Grief reminds you of the gifts you still have, that time and love are everything, and that you should never waste a moment.

Chapter 13: Moving Out

This door is multi-colored, it balances between being extremely dark and light. I know that it has multiple layers. This door will lead me to a series of doors, ones that are ready to be closed and ones that are dying to be opened. I enter the first, it is the door at our house on Bear Dance. The brown color warms me, it is a door that I will soon have to close and say goodbye to.

"I am selling the house," my mom told me a few weeks after Ryan passed, "I just can't live here anymore. Every time I leave, I pass his house and I picture the ambulance outside on the street and I just can't do it anymore."

"Okay," I responded, dragging out the "kay" sending the message that I was unsure of what came next.

I didn't really know what to say.

"We're moving. I found a two-bedroom house, it's really nice, just a lot smaller than what we are used to" she said quickly.

But there are four of us, I thought to myself silently.

Through all the chaos of Scott being sick and Ryan passing away, my mother adopted two little boys through foster care. It was something she started doing when it was just her and I left at home.

We went through many different kids, all aged around three to eight. All of them were so dang sweet and deserving of so much more. It was never a permanent plan, just something my mom was doing. That was the case at least, until she got the call in 2009. There was a brand-new baby in the NICU who needed a home. As soon as she saw him, she knew that she wanted to keep him. So, as soon as the hospital released him, she began raising him as her own and we became a house of three. And when the state called that he had a little brother a few years later in 2011, she would take him in too, making us a house of four.

She knew the importance of having a sibling and she wanted to give the boys the same gift that she had given the five of us. Especially because by the time he was three years old, all of us siblings had already moved out. So, in 2013, seven months after Ryan passed, my mom officially adopted another son.

I was sixteen when she adopted the first, and nineteen when she adopted the second. I felt indifferent to it all. With everything going on between Scott's cancer, losing Ryan, leaving my relationship, and starting therapy, I didn't have much emotional capacity left. My heart wasn't exactly open at the time, nor was I ready to have two new brothers when I had just lost one of mine and the other one's life was up in the air.

The boys she adopted are amazing and I love them wholeheartedly, but at the time I was doing it from a distance. There was nothing wrong with the situation, it was just a lot to take on top of it all. I was in my healing era, and I was on a mission to get through it.

My identity as the last of five seemed confusing now. Because within a few years, we went from five to four and now to six. It just didn't feel like what I knew to be true. My entire growing-up identity as a baby was still my reality and now everything I knew was a blur.

It often felt like this time was split into a before and after. There was our before family, my mom plus us five. Then, there was our after family, the new one she would create as we grew up and left to make our own.

I knew that her moving into this smaller house was just another step into her after-family. It meant me moving out and moving on. I was eighteen, so the time was coming anyways.

It just came faster than I was prepared for. Throughout the tornado of constant change, moving into my own place wasn't even on my mind.

"You can always come with us, we can make it work," my mom told me.

But, I knew there was no room for me. It was easier for everyone if I just went somewhere else.

I could technically go live at my dad's house, but other than his girlfriend, it was completely empty. Scott and my dad were living in Texas full time and a three-story house to myself sounded just as lonely as it did scary.

I got along with his girlfriend, but since Ryan died, she hasn't really approved of my decisions. At eighteen, I felt betrayed as she told my dad all the disappointing things I was doing. I couldn't live there with her. I needed more secrecy as I navigated through my grief.

That's why, after my mom told me, I went for a drive. I wanted to get away from it for a while. I wanted to be able to react in the privacy of my car, in Karen. That way, I didn't have to feel guilty for the big emotions that were coming over me. I pulled over as I felt the tears approaching making it harder and harder to see.

I picked up my phone and called Kendra "I have nowhere to go" I sobbed to her.

I knew why my mom had to move. I knew why my dad couldn't be home with me. I knew deep down that my dad's girlfriend loved me and that she was just worried. I knew I was lucky to be healthy. To be alive. I knew a lot of the things I was doing were my fault and making things worse. But I shoved all of that stuff down out of my awareness, to the point where all I knew was that I was in pain.

I felt so abandoned. So alone. So chucked to the side, as if no one cared about what happened to me. I am aware enough now to know that this sounds dramatic, but it is genuinely how I felt at the time, and I felt guilty for feeling it. I felt selfish.

"Come live with me," my sister Kendra responded.

"Are you serious?"

"Yeah, my roommate just moved out. You would only need to help with the rent. I know how it is to feel like you have nowhere to go, but I want you to know that you do have somewhere. You always have somewhere with me," she said.

I shut the brown door, waved goodbye, and opened the yellow one in front of me.

The bright yellow paint was chipping from the wood and it offered me something new. Something light. Something warm. I grabbed onto the black door handle and as soon as I swung it open, Kendra was right there waiting for me.

Kendra gave me so much more than a place to stay that day. She gave me a safe space to figure out my life. She gave me a supportive, calm environment where she could model to me the wonders of adulthood.

She gave me guidance. She gave me unconditional love. She gave me a home. And for the entire year that I would live here, I would slowly, but surely turn my entire life around for the better. It would be my stepping stone for the rest of my life. Partly because my sister wouldn't put up with anything less, but also because she showed me that I had to start fighting for the life that I wanted.

My favorite part about our sister townhouse was that my sister had her art hung up on the walls. Her paintings paired with the concrete floors mimicked the undeniable beauty of simple things. Our house was nearly empty, we didn't have a lot of stuff inside.

As I walk through the front door, I see her art on the wall on my right. I run my hands over the paintings, I cannot believe she can create things that look like this.

On my left is our living room. It houses one yellow couch and a lot of books that fill our black bookshelves. It fits us both perfectly. If one was to explore our bookshelves, they would find only fiction or fantasy, they are our favorite. When we aren't reading *Harry Potter*, we are searching for the next book like it.

Fantasy novels have such a way with the brain. They provide such an escape. Something both of us find ourselves craving. We spent a lot of nights reading together on that yellow leather couch.

As I sit on this couch today, I catch myself staring into her paintings on our wall. I can see where each stroke is placed with a delicate hand. I love to see her work hung up in our home. It makes me feel proud. She often hides it away, she somehow doesn't see what I do. I wonder if she knows how much it means to me, the hope her art makes me feel.

Especially the drawing I pulled out from under a stack of others that lay on her desk. I saw the eye in the corner of the photo, an eye I knew too well. It was Ryan. I gently pulled the drawing out to reveal the most insanely realistic drawing I had ever seen. It was my brother smiling and next to him was his son, our nephew. *How have none of us seen this?* I gently put it back where it was and waited for her to show me when she was ready. I decided I had been nosey enough for one day.

Kendra is an insanely talented artist, but she'll never admit it. Both of my sisters are actually. That was not a gift that was passed down to me.

For my mom's fiftieth birthday, Kendra painted her a picture of me. It was a gift, that would eventually be stolen by me. It was a gift that, even though it was not for me, meant more to me than anyone could possibly know. What a beautiful thing to see yourself through someone else's eyes.

The painting she did of me will forever be one of my favorite things. One, because of the way she painted me, the way she sees me. The way it contains and emulates light is something that I have forgotten I have. The bright yet mustard yellow background, the side profile of my face, head thrown back carelessly, the lip-closed smirk I always have, my long black hair flowing up all around me, and the five red roses placed throughout it.

The five, just like the five of us.

In many ways, whether intentional or not, the painting symbolized all my siblings with me. The way that they always were. I always felt like I had a little bit of all of them in me. It symbolized the freedom I wish I felt. This girl looked like she was made for letting go, facing fears, chasing dreams. It was perfect. It was who I wished to be. It just wasn't me, yet. She painted me as the woman I could become.

While we lived together, we did most of our bonding on our bar stools. Eating junk food, indulging in wine, talking about everything and anything, and constantly sharing our truths. We became so close. No one would even know that as kids, we kind of hated each other. "But look at us, now," we would remind ourselves.

I forgave her for bullying me through Barbies and she forgave me for all the hateful sticky notes I would leave on her door. We were grown women now, we were past it. I even forgave her for praying that I would get kidnapped, but only because she promised that she included "by a good family" in that prayer. Even at our worst, we siblings looked out for each other.

By the time I moved in with my sister, I had been in therapy for about a year, so most of our conversations revolved around all the things that were coming up for me. Depending on what room I ventured into that day, she always had different ways of cheering me up. We talked a lot about Ryan and how much we missed him. We shared our favorite memories and the heaviness of our grief.

We talked a lot about Scott and we spent a lot of our time praying over him and his cancer. We prayed that he would make it through this, we prayed that we would make it through this, and we prayed that we would not lose another brother. We prayed for peace as we knew his next PET scan was coming.

I carefully pushed the yellow door shut.

Chapter 14: Moving On

Sitting here in therapy, I am happy to include my therapist in the news of Scott's cancer-free scan. She's been going through all this with me, so it feels good to bring in happier news. It's not usually that way in here. Although a lot of joy has been felt on this couch, mostly it has been a safe spot to shed my grief.

Today the room feels just a little lighter and all I want to do is walk in through the yellow-chipped-paint door that will take me to my sister.

I close my eyes to picture it, and the second I turn the handle I see on the clock that it is two in the morning and Kendra will not stop talking about how good Mexican food sounds. We have been talking all night and the mascara streaks down our faces make us look a little crazy, but a lot more real. We've been sitting at our bar top for hours. We're trying to be positive, to be happy that Scott's cancer is gone. But really, we're just letting our guards down, we're letting it all pour out. Everything we kept inside for the last three years is beginning to surface and it's coming out in bursts of laughter and tears.

We talk about ex-boyfriends and wonder how we ever lost ourselves in someone else. We come to so many conclusions, so many answers, but in the end, we know that we chased what we saw. What we saw at home, on TV, what we read in books. All of those love stories were packed full of drama, toxic patterns, and so much lust. But none of those things were love, not the kind we wanted anyway. So, we decided to change what we were going to look for because we finally understood that what we want is something we have never seen before.

We cry over Ryan and all the missed moments and memories. She tells me all about her adult relationship with him, the one I envy because it was one I could never get. He died before I became one. I am still becoming one.

We cry about how lonely and lost we felt through Scott's illness. How the revolving door of worry, pain, and guilt never ends. We cry about how he must feel. How we struggle to admit our pain as we watch how much he suffered. When we watch him continue to suffer.

We talked about our stepfather, and we realized we had more in common than we knew. We spill the secrets we have been holding in for over a decade. It feels so good.

And now, we laugh until we cry while we ride in her car and drive twenty minutes away from our house to the only disgusting Mexican restaurant that is still open at two in the morning.

* * *

It feels good to have someone to rely on. A sibling to come home to. Being the youngest of five, I had to watch as all four of them grew up and left home. It was hard to be left behind. It was hard to stay home without them. It was hard to move on.

To be back in a house with one of them now felt like everything to me. Siblings have such a special place in our hearts. It's someone who isn't a parent, so they aren't controlling over you. They are family and a friend. They aren't going to be on board with anything less than good for you. And if they are going to let you make a bad decision, they are not going to let you do it without them. They are always there when you need love, not judgment. Acceptance, not criticism. Whether right next to you on a chair or on the phone a whole state away. When you need your siblings, they are there. At least mine are. Someone who you can have so much fun with, but someone who is also willing to call you on your crap when you need it. The best part about my family is how tight the five kids have always been. We were each other's lifelines and living with Kendra was exactly what I needed.

Everything started to clear up in 2013. I could finally see that so many tough moments and odd turns had led me here, it is exactly where I needed to be. It is a place where I can grow.

"Ashleigh! I have news! Where are you?" Kendra came through our front door yell-singing. She does this a lot. Yell-sings. She's honestly not bad at it.

"In here Krawna!" I shouted back from my room.

"Guess what?" she asked me.

I lift my eyebrows the way I always do, "Spit it out, dude."

"I have a boyfriend," she said with a sly smile across her face.

"Weird," I replied.

"Rude," she responded.

"No, it's just weird because I got a boyfriend today too," I quietly say in disbelief "What are the odds" I followed with a wink.

After we both left our toxic situations, we thought we would be together forever. Single sisters for life. Living it up in our townhouse, perhaps get a slew of cats. But here we were, on the same exact day, we started dating our future husbands. We just didn't know it.

Chapter 15: Meeting the One

How could I have known it? Truthfully, the first time I met my husband was in 2012 right after I lost my brother. I was a hot mess. And he was a hot nun. It was Halloween and maybe it's because I grew up Catholic, but that nun costume he was in, was really doing it for me. That, and the fact that he was nothing like anyone I had dated before. He was different in all the ways I hoped he would be. But I wasn't different, not yet. I wasn't ready to love someone like him, I had more work to do on me. This was a door I was proud to go in. This was a door that represented redemption and change.

When I open it, I immediately can picture us both awkwardly staring at each other from across the room at multiple parties. Every time I run into him, it is the same.

There is such a strong pull to him. One, that we both fight strongly against. One night, after perhaps a few too many drinks, I stumbled over feeling very cool, and I sat next to him on the couch. The party is full, but all I can see is him. He's keeping to himself, hanging out on the couch, and I am so drawn to it. He looks so coy over there, like he is just waiting for me.

I want to know him. It is my chance, I convince myself. I take a seat right next to him.

"Oh, you're cute" I mumble out.

Cute, I think *Oh no*. I place my head in my hand, trying to play it off, looking down at my feet. I had a grand plan of saying something smooth, but the words just fell out. Those freckles get the best of me. When I look up at him, his cheeks are red and he is grinning, so I know I at least make an impression.

"And you are trouble" he says back to me.

He places his hand on my leg, but only for a second. He stands up and walks away. *Wow. Way smoother than me*, I sit down and wonder how I am going to play this.

After two years of "accidentally" bumping into each other, and two years of flirting going nowhere, the pull is still there, but for some reason that I didn't understand, neither one of us was pushing too hard to pursue it. We know we have a connection. We knew it as soon as we met. It was undeniable, the chemistry overwhelmed me in all the ways you want it to.

The second time I see him, he kisses me. I am in the middle of a sentence when he leans in and goes for it. I pull away from the surprise, bite my bottom lip, and question.

"Did you really just kiss me?"

"Uhh, yeah. I guess I did" he laughs in return.

It won't take us anywhere just yet, but it will become a sweet memory. I can't believe he has the nerve to interrupt me with a kiss. I can't believe how much I enjoyed it. He is bold and I am so into it.

The first time I laid eyes on that man, I knew that one day, he would mean so much to me. I could feel it down to my bones, to my core, it was the truth. The timing wasn't right until it was. I wasn't ready for him until I was. I will forever be grateful that we didn't start dating until 2014 when we both were ready to be good for each other.

The timing was everything, I wanted to make sure I mastered the right person-right time rule. Unfortunately, our timing for love was a bit dark, but it happened exactly when it needed to.

We had something terrible in common, something that would bring us together another time. We had a mutual friend pass away and I didn't expect to run into him at the funeral, or at the after-celebration of her life, but here he was.

My head is sick with sadness. I am not in a place where I am looking for love. I am in shock trying to navigate more grief. I don't feel like I have room for much more. I am just happy to see a face I enjoy on such a horrible night. A distraction that I am ready to welcome.

The after-celebration of her life turns into quite the show. A lot of drinking, a lot of emotions. But tonight, I am not partaking in the party. I am there to support my friends and to celebrate the life of a friend, and drinking sounds like a terrible idea to me. So many people who love her are here, and it is a full-on emotional warfare in this house. People seem to be crying in every corner.

I hung my head low. But, when I hear the front door open, I curiously look over to see who is joining.

"Crap," I say to my friend as I point to the door, "Cody's here. I'm going to call for a ride home. I don't want to be here if he is."

I walk quickly into the filthy kitchen in hopes that he doesn't see me. I lean back and pull myself onto the counter in the corner to sit in what I hope is out of sight. I immediately pulled out my phone to text my mom. My hands are shaking. I know I have to get out of here fast. I started typing the message, but that's when I heard it, when I heard him.

"Hey," he says as he walks up to me.

I don't look up. Maybe if I pretend like I don't know he is here or that he is talking to me, he will go away. Could I get that lucky?

"You know what's great about us?" he says as he looks around to make sure everyone is watching.

I look up at him with just my eyes, hoping he can read my so-not-in-the-mood face.

"We can still do this," he says as he grabs the back of my head and pulls it down to his for an unwanted kiss.

I turn my head away from him instantly and pull back. Only he would want to humiliate me at a time like this. Only he would think that he could get away with something like this after two years of me avoiding him. At a party after my friend had just died.

"Just leave me alone," I say slowly jumping down from the counter.

I picked up my pace, trying to put some more distance between us. I force my way through the crying crowd and go into the first empty room I can find. I try to catch my breath and get my head straight. I practice breathing as my therapist taught me, I try to slow my thoughts down. My fear feels like it is swimming around me, trying to pull me in and I am doing everything I can to fight against it. To not let him win.

Once I feel a little calmer, I pull out my phone again to call my mom. I just want her to come and get me, but before I can get her number dialed, the door opens behind me. It feels like going back in time because I have been here so many times before. I feel him grab onto me before I can even turn around. He grabs my head and starts trying to kiss me again, he tries to kiss my neck as I use both of my hands to push him away. I was going to fight back this time.

There is no one here to help me, but I am ready to do whatever it is going to take. He is seriously drunk, and I am thoroughly grossed out and getting more and more uncomfortable. I keep shrugging him off and telling him to stop, but each time I do, he tries that much harder to get his way. He hasn't changed. But I have.

I am not the girl he knew two years ago. That girl is so long gone and so far behind me. I am not the girl who is small, spit on, or taken advantage of. I am not the girl who is going to let any man ignore my no. I am not the girl I used to be, and I will never be her again. I am not a kid anymore.

I see him through the crack in the door, walking past. I see the flat-billed hat that covers his brown hair and his black rectangle-framed glasses that sit underneath. The only thing that stood in front of his intoxicating blue eyes and my sanity. I see him and in my head, I beg him to look at me.

The second he does, I yell his name, "Will!"

He jerks his head to me even more. He opens the door the

rest of the way and he looks confused as to why I just called him in here. He looks confused as to why I am crying and why Cody is acting like this. Few would see this side of him, only the girls he traumatized and the few others that would witness it.

"Help me" I mouth to him over my ex's shoulder.

I don't want to cause a scene, not today.

Will immediately steps up and reaches for me. He takes my hand in his, and I never want to feel him let go. He quickly yet gently pulls me out of there and gets Cody to back off.

Will and I walk out, hand in hand. He pulls me through the crowd and towards the front door. We came in barely friends, but we would be leaving together. Cody wasn't going to give up that easily, it wasn't in his nature. He follows us out of the party and all the way out to the car. Screaming at us both, cussing at us both the whole way.

"You're really going to leave with this guy?" he yells into the car window as we prepare to drive away.

I look at Will with my big brown eyes and a smirk on my face, "Yeah, I finally am" I reply.

* * *

This room with the yellow door marks an important era of my life. One of growth, change, and confidence. I was becoming more like the version of myself from the portrait that my sister Kendra painted. And I was letting go of the person I became to cope with the trauma I endured. My sister offered me a safe and healthy environment to become who I was supposed to become.

I still had a ways to go, but I finally liked who I was becoming. And I started feeling more comfortable in myself and my decisions. I finally started to feel like I deserved better than how I was treated in my past relationships. Grief was still present but not all-consuming. I had been drowning for so long but now my head was above the water and I was excited to see where this new room might lead.

Chapter 16:
Bumps on the Road

The joy and sadness twirl together in a dance. This door will lead me to one of the happiest discoveries of my life. The news would come when I would need it most, when I was begging for something good, something to live for. As I sit here, the emotions stay at the front of my mind and I cannot deny or push them down. They are too strong, too deep. The door is heavy and wide. It is sterile and windowless. It is ready to be opened. I turn the handle, hear a click and force it open.

It is the night before Easter. I am getting ready to go to bed and I'm excited. I have finally met someone who I am proud to bring home to my family. I cannot get it out of my mind, to the point that even as I drift off to sleep, I dream of the holiday. In my dream, all of us are together. Every holiday is spent the same way. We all meet at my grandmother's at noon, she hosts at her lovely house on her farm. We eat a turkey that my mother has made. The smells alone probably have me drooling in my sleep. My mom is an excellent cook. The meat would pair exactly right with the special green beans that my aunt always made. The ones that were mixed with some tomato concoction and tiny slices of bacon.

As we walk in the back door upon arrival, we are greeted with a hug and a kiss from my grandmother who feels so tiny in my arms. I would hold on a little tighter, a little longer each year that passed. My grandmother is one of my absolute best friends, someone who could always make me feel seen and loved.

As we stand and sit around her kitchen island, I tell all the women in my family about the boy I am falling in love with.

We tend to be one of those families who tell each other everything, so I am happy to dump out the information as they ask me, "So, Ash what's new?"

My time is limited on holidays because I have to split them up. So, while my grandma's starts at noon, I am usually there by eleven. I want to soak up all the time I can get with my mom's side. Because once it gets close to two, Scott and I will need to leave.

We will kiss and hug everyone goodbye and ride together to my dad's. This is how we do it. We ride in his car with the rap music turned up way too loud, and we sing and drop beats the whole way there. We split every holiday. It was hard to fathom not seeing everyone. So instead of doing every other, we do them all halfway.

As we drive, I finally muster up some courage. I turn down the stereo to put Mike Jones on hold for a sec. I want to tell Scott about Will before we get to our dads.

In my dream, his reaction tells me everything I need to know. I cannot believe that this will be the very first time in history that I will tell him who I am dating, and he will have a positive reaction to it. He usually has something like "You can do way better" or "Are you stupid?" to say. While it sounds harsh, he doesn't mean it to be. It's out of love and I know that.

When I told him about Cody for the first time, he got so pissed that he didn't say anything at all. He got up from the table, leaving uneaten dinner, and shook his head as he walked off. That felt even worse. I would have preferred a rude comment.

While I knew it was his way of showing protection, it usually just made me feel like he was right. I was stupid. Because for some reason I wasn't attracted to good things, but I didn't know how to change that. I wasn't mad at him for it, but I kept getting disappointed in myself.

In my truth- I attracted what I was- which meant, I didn't think I was that good either. But, that wasn't my truth now.

Deep in my heart, I prayed for Scott to be happy when I told him. I convinced myself that if he was- that meant Will was the one. It would confirm what I already knew. So, when I told him in my dream and he smiled and said, "I'm happy for you" I would wake up chasing that reality.

Once I told Scott anything, I was on a ticking time clock before he would tell my father, so I planned to be quick about it. Right after we arrived, I would walk in, greet the family and tell him. My dad was a lot easier to tell these things to than my brother in these moments. He didn't worry about it as much as Scott did. He mostly just was happy for me and I think deep down he had a lot of faith that I would eventually figure things out on my own. Probably because he saw what everyone else did in me, I was a lot like him.

* * *

This Easter wouldn't follow the patterns of the past, nor would it come close to this dream. I would wake up from a beautiful dream to be greeted by a nightmare. The sun wouldn't wake us on this faithful day, but darkness would.

Because the night before Easter my brother laid out his outfit and went to bed and when he woke up in the morning, it would be a whole month later.

He was rushed to the emergency room in the middle of the night and put into a medically induced coma, none of which he remembered. He woke up very confused that he wasn't at home, it wasn't Easter, and his baby sister was standing next to him with an ever-growing round little bump of a belly. He went to sleep without even knowing I had a boyfriend, and he woke up to this.

Being pregnant at nineteen was a shock enough for my family, but it was more shocking to wake up from a coma without a single warning. And while that little belly scared the crap out of us all, it ended up changing and reshaping our family forever for the better.

Growing up Catholic, I understood the whole baby out-of-wedlock thing was not ideal. That I was supposed to feel guilty for my sin. That I should be ashamed of myself. But what I was so unaware of was that it was ideal for me. There was no shame here. And I was okay with this sin because it gave me the one thing I had been praying to have for years, *courage*. While it was never my daughter's job, nor our intention, getting pregnant with her would bring a new woman out of me. A better one.

Scott isn't awake for long before they have to put him back under. They use machines to keep his body working so he can rest while they attempt to heal his lungs.

He won't wake up again until later in May and this time he won't be able to speak because of the tube they have placed in his throat. I watch as they weaned him off his medication and he slowly begins to wake up and open his eyes. The nurse stops him as his hand reaches up to his throat where a tube is now placed inside.

It takes him a few minutes to realize that he cannot speak, but it takes him almost no time to look up and see the date written on the calendar on the wall in front of him. It is May 25, 2014.

He reaches to his bedside table for his little whiteboard with weak shaking hands, and I watch as he writes. When he finishes, he flips it over to me and tries to smile.

"Happy Birthday."

It is scribbled roughly, but I can tell what it says. I just can't believe he did it. I smile and wipe a tear from my eyes. Today, I am twenty.

Scott hadn't lifted a finger or used a muscle in a little over a month, so it was barely legible, but I knew my brother and I knew what it said. I gave him the softest hug I could, worried that he was too fragile to even touch, and then I gestured at my pregnant belly and lifted my eyebrows. Then, he drew a scribble smile.

This was the last time I would see him awake for months. As I watched my brother lie in that hospital bed, only being kept alive by machines, I quickly realized that cancer wasn't going to be the worst thing he went through. This was.

From the lack of movement, his body became so swollen it looked like his skin was going to burst at any moment. He was retaining so much water that it looked like he had gained fifty pounds. His lips became dry and cracked from being opened around a ventilator tube twenty-four-seven. And his skin became stretched and pulled in every direction.

As he lay lifeless in that bed, I would put lotion on his arms and hands in hopes of easing his skin as it stretched to accommodate the swelling. I would put chapstick on his lips in hopes of minimizing the cracking. I would do anything small that I could just to feel like I was helping in some way. As small and insignificant as these things seem, it was something, the only thing, that I could do.

It was something other than just sitting by his hospital bed, rubbing my growing belly and hoping and wishing and praying that he would be here and be awake when my baby was born.

After my brother's stem cell transplant, he had to be on immunosuppressants, which are exactly what they sound like. They suppress your immune system, putting you at a higher risk of getting ill. They do this to help your body not fight back or reject your life-saving transplant. Which is great, but it also means that your body cannot fight back as well as it should against anything else either.

Scott was outside his house, moving a grill when it happened.

My pocket started vibrating and when I lifted it up to my

ear I immediately heard "I'm just calling because I need your help. Scott fell and hurt his knee and we are headed to the emergency room now," said my mom.

"Alright, I will meet you there."

"Please let your dad know," she said as she hung up the phone.

I called my father on the way to the hospital, it wasn't a route I had to pay much attention to. I have done this drive over a hundred times just in all the visits to see my brother.

When I arrived, I was quickly taken back by a nurse who showed me the way to Scott. They were in one of the back areas in the Emergency department as the nurse and doctor worked together to wrap up his knee. I am assuming they did other things, but all I can remember was how gigantic it was. It freaked me out.

His knee was massive and looked like something out of a horror movie. It was incredibly swollen, and my brother was wincing in pain as he held it. I let myself relax and breathe easy. This was just an injury, one he would quickly recover from, so there was nothing to worry about. But with my brother, there is always something to worry about. I was being naive. Purposely.

While the cancer was gone, his struggles, his worries, and his suffering were not. He was looking and acting more like himself since the treatments stopped, but he wasn't granted this grace for long. What started as a fall and an injured knee became an infection. The infection led to a lengthy hospital stay and it became an infection that would soon begin to attack his lungs. When I tell you I thought cancer was the #1 enemy, I meant it, but man, was I wrong. When an infection hits your vital organs, it's a whole other ballgame.

The antibiotics could not seem to kill the pseudomonas that invaded his lungs. Nothing they threw at it was working. The doctors began to run out of medicine, out of answers, out of hope. It was known that if we could not find a treatment, and soon, we would lose this battle. They decided the best option, the only option, was to medically induce a coma while they searched for a cure. They needed machines to do the heavy lifting, so my brother's body could rest as they attempted to find a way to heal his lungs. A swollen knee? Seriously? That's how we got here?

As I sat at the foot of my brother's hospital bed, I found it extremely hard to look him in the eyes. He is so skinny and frail under those thin white blankets that you could barely distinguish that a body was underneath. I reached up for his hand and just held it in a peaceful silence. I squeezed it tightly as I stared down at it, begging my brain to remember every inch of his hand. To remember everything about him and the way it felt to have his hand in mine.

I knew the worst-case scenario here. I had done it already. My memories of Ryan have faded over time. I struggle to picture him at times, to picture his hands, to remember his voice and what it felt like when he hugged me. I didn't want to take this time with Scott for granted, I didn't want the memories to fade. I wanted to keep them with me. So, I held on, and I promised not to forget.

I finally gathered up the courage to look up at Scott and tried to take it all in. As painful as it was, I never wanted to forget this moment. I felt my tears slide from my cheek and watched them fall onto our hands. Together we sat in the somehow loudest yet silent room, filled with the horrific worries of what we feared could come.

"I'm so glad you are awake now," I whispered.

"I missed so much," he said tilting his chin up gesturing towards my now very round belly.

"At least you are here now" I reminded him.

'"I have to make it to December. I have to meet her," he said, his voice cracking as he tried to hold back tears of his own.

"You will, you don't have a choice. She is going to need her Uncle Scotty," I mumbled back. It was hard to get the words out. As each one came out of my mouth, the lump in my throat tripled in size. The gravity that he may not make it to meet my daughter crushed me. I was struggling enough to accept that she was already missing out on one incredible uncle. Thinking of her missing out on two felt unbearable to me. He was her only uncle left, by blood anyway.

Every time I felt excited about this pregnancy, there was always sadness there. Ryan wasn't going to be here for this. It was hard to accept that he would never hold his own niece. My brain couldn't even process the reality that the odds were against us. If the doctors were right, Scott would never hold her either.

Chapter 17:
Learning to Never Give Up

The conference room was meant for privacy. The kind of privacy you would need to let a family know that their loved one was not going to make it. So why were all the walls glass? That was the main thought running through my head as we walked in the door. The glass walls offered privacy from the sounds, but they offered zero discretion for the suffering we were about to display.

"Hey girls, the doctor wants to discuss something with the family in the conference room regarding Scott. It's important that everyone is there," my dad said firmly.

We went in with our whole family: my father, my mother, my two sisters, and I. I sat down next to my sister Kendra in an uncomfortable chair at the oval table. It looked like a place for business meetings. I put my elbows up and placed my head in my hands. I knew what was coming. We all did.

In this room, we were told that we needed to prepare ourselves for the worst.

"It is time to consider ending lifesaving care and perhaps just focus on making Scott comfortable," the doctor said slowly. The treatments weren't working and we knew that. They were out of options, and he was dying a little more every day. It was clear that whatever my brother was struggling with, this hospital didn't know how to deal with it.

"So, they just give up?" I asked my dad, giving him a pissed-off tone that he knew wasn't meant for him.

"I will never give up" he reminded me with a wink. He picked up his phone and made a call.

My mother had to absorb the fact that in her lifetime, she may lose both of her sons. My sisters and I, to lose both of our brothers. And my father lost a stepson he loved and now he risked losing a son of his very own. It felt unfair, like for some reason my family kept getting tested, but we were just not receiving the message.

My father walked in a little while later, "MD Anderson has an idea. It's an antibiotic that was pulled off the shelf, but it was used in the past in treating pseudomonas. Have you tried that?" He asked Scott's doctor.

Their faces looked a sort of shameful surprise, "Well, no we haven't. They pulled that drug off the shelves a long time ago."

"Well, his doctors in Houston said we should try it, so let's see how it goes" my father responded, in his cavalier tone that he always had, but still people knew that he meant business.

When the doctors lost hope, my father supplied enough for us all. He called major hospitals and demanded help in searching for innovative ideas, recent technology, new medicine, old medicine, experimental medicine, whatever it took. He was not about to roll over and give up. He was the strength, the force, the brain power that we needed.

He did everything you would hope your doctors would. He found the answer in hours, and they were just going to let a twenty-something kid die. That is when I learned the importance of never giving up, never accepting anything at face value, never backing down, and never losing faith.

My father is a man of many talents, but he is the humblest person I know. He would never tell you that he played in the NFL as a quarterback, that he came from very humble beginnings and built an incredible life. He would not complain about a thing. He would not talk poorly about anyone or make any excuses. He would just work hard and get things done. I admired him so much. I look up to him so much.

On this day, he, with the help of M.D Anderson, saved Scott's life.

It took one hospital's idea of using an old drug that had been pulled off the shelf, and within two days that antibiotic was working. In just 48 hours, we went from a death sentence to a cure that could stop the infection in its tracks and prevent any further damage from happening.

His lungs suffered greatly, and the scarring and damage left behind could not be fixed or undone. The antibiotics could stop the spread of the infection, but they could not repair the loss of lung function that occurred. We were made painfully aware that at just twenty-five years old my brother would be on oxygen for the rest of his life. And eventually, if the lungs began to worsen, which they likely would, he would need a double lung transplant. So spins the revolving door that we can never get out of.

Scott finally left the hospital and things began to get somehow normal again. At least, a new normal. Scott had to get used to living his life in a completely different light. He had been bedridden for months and could not roll out of bed by himself anymore. He moved into my dad's house until he could begin taking care of himself again.

My dad's house had three floors, and all of the bedrooms were either up or down, so knowing Scott could barely walk, my dad made him a bedroom in the dining room to make things easier. I moved back in with my dad as well. This way, I could help Scott and save money before I had the baby.

As much as I loved living with my sister Kendra in our very own little house, I needed to start planning for the future. My sister and I were so happy and so close there, those memories carried me through so many dark rooms. But it was time for me to work towards being on my own and finding myself a home to bring my daughter into. My dad needed help with my brother, and I needed help with my future. It made sense.

We worked together in nursing Scott back to some version of his past self. We would help him sit up until slowly he gained the muscle to do it himself again. We would help him walk and encourage him to take as many steps as he could on his own until he would eventually walk again without needing us for support. His strength returned to him slowly, but it came in incredibly gratifying strides. Watching a grown man learn how to walk was an incredible joy I had no idea existed. Watching him master all these firsts gave me a glimpse of what it would feel like when I watched my daughter sit up, crawl, and take a step for the first time. Finding joy in these tiny things became so easy. There are so many things we can do that we forget to be thankful for. I was becoming more grateful.

"Hey, could you help me wrap my port so I can take a shower?" my brother asked me.

Every time he asked me for help with anything medical, he did so like he was afraid to be a bother.

I grabbed the saran wrap and carefully and meticulously wrapped it around his arm and his chest in hopes of keeping it in place. It sat just under his collarbone, and it looked extremely uncomfortable. This was ironic because its purpose was to help with comfort in hopes of limiting the number of pokes he would endure as they were constantly shoving medicine into it.

He smiled at me graciously and I helped him stand up so he could work his way to the shower. As soon as I heard the water turn on, I turned the volume off on the TV. I knew he had a chair in there so he could sit through it, but I wanted to make sure if he fell or any worrisome sounds came out, that I could make sure I heard them and ensure his safety.

He came out about half an hour later. It took a lot out of him to shower and get dressed. He grabbed a couple of syringes out of his fridge and walked up to me with a guilty expression for needing my help again.

I loved helping him. I knew he hated it, but it made me feel needed and right now that meant a lot to me. Looking down at my growing stomach, I knew I was going to be a lot less help to him soon when the baby arrived, so I wanted to help as much as I could before she got here.

I took the syringes and unscrewed the orange caps. One syringe at a time, I slowly but surely pushed the medicine into his port with delicate and nervous hands in hopes that I wasn't causing him discomfort. I wondered what it felt like, but would never ask. Neither one of us talked about his illness with the other, we just repeatedly told each other, "I love you" and "It's going to be okay."

He began to cough, so aggressively, he had this cough attack often. I jumped up from the couch and waddled to the counter so I could grab him a bag to spit in. He was always coughing up so much stuff out of his lungs. It looked and sounded just as painful as I'm sure it felt. We were repeatedly reminded that this part would never get better. The lung damage was done and other than a transplant, there wasn't much they could do to offer him relief or improvement.

The one thing he did to make sure to improve was his strength. He took it in a small and consistent stride, it would take time to rebuild an entire body after months of being stuck in a bed. But we were on a timeline. My pregnancy was coming to a close and he needed to be at least strong enough to hold a baby by December.

"You know if I make it, you have to let me be the first one to hold her," he told me.

I grabbed his hand. "You will make it, and you can be the first, right after Will and me," I said with a smile.

I almost believed it. It was a future I would beg for. He squeezed my hand tighter, and the biggest tear fell down my cheek. I looked away to hide it. I'll save it for the car, I thought. I wanted to be strong for him.

Sometimes, I wonder if being strong sends the wrong message. Like crying about this wasn't okay. Maybe he should have seen us wail and cry the way that we all did. That way he would have known he could do it too. He had every right, and it might have helped him feel less alone if we didn't tip-toe around him all the time. Maybe he needed to see us show as much sadness as he felt.

* * *

This room held so much joy and pain simultaneously. I loved the life I was building with Will, as unconventional as it was, and I was so excited to meet my baby girl. I think back on the dream I had before Easter, pre-pregnancy, and telling Scott about Will and how happy I knew he would be at that news. Life has never gone the way I pictured or planned. There have always been curve balls and bumps in the road that have at times knocked me off course and knocked me to my knees.

I knew this was a door I couldn't completely close, and I didn't want to. This room, this season taught me how to hold joy and pain simultaneously and not let one override the other. This room taught me just how strong hope is and to never give up even when you receive the worst news imaginable. And though I didn't need a reminder of just how strong my family was, it was a trait that was once again revealed in this room. I was reminded of how much I relied on my family to be my strength, and how grateful I was to walk through life with them.

Chapter 18: Surrendering Perfect

Looking at my therapist now, I wonder if she knows that I have news. That I have something to tell her that is major. I assume she knows all my "tells" by now because everyone says I am incredibly easy to read.

Oddly enough, the door is a bathroom stall. It is navy and it is cheap, but when I open it, the other side of the door contains a whirlwind of beauty. It is a wallflower and easy to miss at first. What you see at first is not even close to the glory you will get. I run into this room.

It was the last time I would ever be in my car, Karen. I had just picked up a prescription and I was on my way home to the house that I lived in with Kendra. The pill bottle dropped from my hands and rolled onto the floor of my car. I reached for it to try and pick it up, but it slid underneath my brakes. By the time I looked up, it was too late. I threw my arms over my face to shield it as I slammed into the back of a pickup truck.

I woke up in an attack of coughs seconds later. The powder from my airbag felt like it was choking me and it took me a minute to realize that I must have been knocked out for a few seconds. My car was smoking and I was in the middle of the road. I managed to step out and see that my poor car, Karen, the once cherry red G6 that I loved, was a smashed-up pile of junk now. I managed to walk over to the gas station where I ran into the couple that I just hit. They helped me sit down and immediately started wrapping my arm and asking me if I was okay.

How nice are these people? I just hit them and here they are taking care of me. They called the police and I called my mother. I would get a ticket for careless driving, a neck brace, an arm brace, and some pain medication that I would never take.

My mother felt like we should go to the hospital to make sure I was okay. As we sit in the emergency room waiting, a hospital worker comes in and asks to take me back for a scan. They wanted to make sure it was just whiplash and nothing too crazy had happened to my neck. Before he starts the scan, he has me remove all my jewelry and then he asks the question.

"Any chance you could be pregnant?"

"Uh, no?" I said.

Why did I just say that so unsure? Why did that feel like a lie? When was my last period? Oh my god, could I be pregnant?

My mind is racing and he can tell that something is off.

"You know what, let's just put this on you just in case," he says as he drops the lead blanket over my torso to protect me from the radiation.

When we check out of the hospital, my mother is brave enough to offer me her car, but instead of driving straight home as I promised, I drive to the store. I had to know what my body already seemed to.

I bought the first pregnancy test I could find and I didn't want to wait until I got home, so I immediately took it in the luxury space of a Walmart bathroom.

I waited standing up, leaning against the germ-infested walls that are public bathrooms. I stared at the test to give me the yes, I already felt to be true.

"Yep, I am pregnant."

My new way of self-soothing since I gave up drinking and terrible decisions, was to take bubble baths. So, when I get home from Walmart, that's exactly what I am going to do.

As soon as I get home, I walk into the bathroom and soak my body in the tub and soak my face with tears. I lay in that tub for a long time, not sure how to feel. *Did I want to be a mom? Would I even be a good one? Was I even worthy of this? How could I make this work?* The questions keep spiraling out of my mind. It is getting harder to breathe. I keep holding my breath and going under the water, hoping to come up to the air to feel just a little less heavy. I feel like I don't know anything, other than the fact that, somehow, I already love this baby.

I must have been crying pretty loudly because my sister just popped the lock and walked in. She sits on the toilet next to me and looks at me the way she does when she demands an answer.

"I'm pregnant" I cry.

"What, Ash?" Kendra asks.

"I am pregnant, and I don't even know if I'll be a good mom. I have to be a good mom if I'm gonna do this."

"The fact that you just found out that you're pregnant, and that's your first thought, ensures that you will be."

"You don't know that."

"But I do," she assures me.

The next morning, I woke up nauseous. My sister was meal-prepping some chicken bright and early as she always did. She was training for a bodybuilding competition, and this was an everyday occurrence. The smell of raw chicken filled my room, and I immediately ran to the bathroom to vomit. This would become my new normal for the next nine months. Waking up to vomit.

I got myself together and went to school anyway. Since I had dropped out of college, I chose to do something busier and more hands-on with my life. Something, if I am being real, that I knew I wouldn't fail at. My stepmom owned a Salon downtown, so it seemed like a good decision. Like the easy thing to do. I knew she would help me through the process and for the sake of honesty, I craved easy. I was tired of things being so damn hard.

College scared me, I never felt good enough to be there, so when the tragedies struck it was easier to just give up. Beauty school gave me the scapegoat I felt I needed.

So, instead of doing nothing, I enrolled myself and got to work. It was not for me, but it was great for me at the time. It kept me busy, allowed me to be artistic, and it gave me a platform to help people in unexpected ways. It truly is amazing what a black salon chair can do for people and their vulnerability, they will tell you anything. I was happy doing hair, but deep down I knew I wanted to help people in a different way. I wanted to help kids, but I didn't know in which capacity yet. I didn't know until I had my daughter.

The smells at the salon are always strong, the piercing scent of pure acetone. The gag-worthy aroma takes over the whole building from a perm. The peroxide mixed with bleach. All of that is covered in layers upon layers of hairspray. It was enough to make you cough, but being pregnant, it was enough to send me. In the first twelve weeks of my pregnancy, I lost nineteen pounds. Nausea felt like it was killing me. Every smell was so overwhelming, and I couldn't keep anything down. So, for the entire pregnancy, I had the luxury of drinking disgusting shakes to help me put on weight.

While my physical health was not at its peak during this time, it was my mental health that scared me the most. I started treating therapy like a race. I was racing to become an *emotionally stable* person before my daughter got here. AKA, in my head, a perfect person. Boy, did I just continue to keep setting myself up for failure? Turns out, perfect isn't an option. So, I gave it my best effort to just give her a mom, who was the best version of me I could be. A version that could deal with her past, to hopefully limit how much of it would leak into our future.

The only thing I was certain of, was that when I saw those two lines on that test, I immediately loved that baby. I was ready to do anything to be better for her.

I called my sister Keena, when I finally finished crying to Kendra as I sat and wallowed in my bath. I was seeking her wisdom, but mostly I just wanted her to comfort me the way that only she can. The second she answered, I just said it. Not even a hello. I just wanted to get it out and what I got in return was exactly why I called. It was exactly what I knew I would get.

The "I love you, no matter what," the "I am here for you, and I will do everything I can to help," and the "You are so amazing Dash, that baby will be so lucky to have you as a mom." She told me everything I was dying to hear. Everything I couldn't tell myself. Everything I feared my boyfriend wouldn't.

My experience with men reminds me not to expect much. So, when it was time to tell my boyfriend, I already had rehearsed what I was going to say. I would go in on the defense and by all means necessary, I would protect my heart. Being the mature nineteen-year-old that I was, I sent him the ever-so-daunting "We need to talk" text. Nothing sends someone down a spiral quite like those words.

He was at the grocery store when I texted him. He knew right away what I had to say. He took the time to go through the store and put everything in his cart back into the correct space. He literally is that good. He was so nervous that he had to leave the store immediately, but he made sure he did it the right way of course. He also made sure to give himself some time to process before he came to see me.

When he got to my house, I opened the door without a word and guided him back to my bedroom. We passed Kendra on the couch, who offered me a sympathetic smile that somehow said, "Good luck."

He sat down on my bed and pressed his back against the headboard without a word. I laid my head on his chest, begging for safety, and quietly let the words come out. It was easier if I didn't have to look at him to see his response.

"I'm pregnant," I said.

"I know," he replied calmly as he wrapped his arm around me.

"You don't have to be a part of this if you don't want to. I can do this on my own, but I thought you should know, I am going to have this baby."

I figured if I beat him to the punch, it wouldn't hurt as bad when he decided to bail on me. That was the reality I was prepared for. That was the reality I was expecting. A young couple gets pregnant, the guy bails, single mom raises the baby on her own. It wasn't a unique story, but to my surprise, that story was not going to be mine.

"I am going to be a part of this" he paused, "I want to be with you" he finished blatantly.

And just for a moment, the universe hugged me. Maybe, I should stop hating surprises.

I didn't know what it felt like to have a partner. To be chosen, to be loved by someone simply because they "wanted to." It felt incredible, but I still didn't trust it. It was so hard for me to trust it. Patterns create trust, and for me, this was so new. This was scarier than the chaotic toxicity I was used to. The one that I could count on, the one that I could trust and bank on 100% always being constant and painful. This new situation felt far riskier. Like each step, I was waiting for the rug to get ripped out from under me, but days turned to weeks, to months, to years, and still, that dark day never came.

The pregnancy was hard on me, my face was full of acne, and I was throwing up every morning. The body changes and the emotional changes begin to take over. The intense urge I felt to literally fix everything wrong with myself before she came out. My therapist told me more than once that I was never going to be issue-less or perfect, but I felt this insane amount of pressure like I just had to be. Like I simply was not good enough to be anyone's mother until I was "fixed" whatever the hell that meant.

* * *

"It's okay ma'am, cussing is allowed on this floor," the nurse told me as I screamed every bad word that I knew. My grandma would be horrified. I gripped the white handles on my hospital bed and wailed. My contractions were only a couple of minutes apart and the breathing exercises were annoying me more than they were helping.

"I can't do this. I'm dying!" I cried to my boyfriend nine months too late.

"Why the heck did I convince myself that I could do this naturally? I couldn't do this naturally! Give me the epidural, please I'm begging you" I pleaded to the nurse, to my boyfriend, to my mom, who were all in the room with me.

"We will have to give you fluids before the epidural, which could take about twenty minutes."

"I can't wait twenty minutes," I interrupted the nurse.

"We can give you pain medication in your IV, that should take the edge off until the anesthesiologist can come in and take care of the epidural" the nurse assured me.

It felt like every bone in my body was breaking to get this baby out, I couldn't take it. The nurse grabbed my arm and flipped it over so she could get to the IV. She pushed the medication in, and the relief immediately came. It was instant and way too strong. It made me feel nothing, except dizziness and confusion.

I reach for my mom's hand. I can barely make out her brown eyes, blonde hair, and tan skin through my blurry vision. I began to cry.

"I am so sorry you had to do this five times, this hurts so bad, thank you for going through this for us," I sobbed.

"Aw, okay baby. It's okay" my mom says as she laughs and brushes my hair back until I finally calm down.

"Wow they gave you something strong" Will says to me.

I just smile and roll my eyes. I have no clue what is happening.

Between the pain, exhaustion, and meds, I am losing my mind. By the time the anesthesiologist comes in I am dilated to an eight, with two centimeters to go, but man I can't hack it.

The nurses sit me up on the edge of the bed and Will stands in front of me. I look into his blue eyes and search for reassurance, which he is struggling to give because he is just as scared as I am. He takes my hands in his and promises me it will be okay.

With my head ducked into his chest, the anesthesiologist struggles to find the perfect moment to insert the needle. They want to do it in between contractions, but mine are almost constant at this point. I feel a slight pinch and it is over. But I can tell by Will's expression that the needle must have been frighteningly large.

Will, who is sweating through not two, but three of his shirts from watching me suffer through my contractions. He is almost as bad off as I am.

"Why are you so sweaty?" I say, frustrated that he keeps leaving my side to change shirts.

"You said you were going to die!" He responds.

I laugh, as I grab his hand. I lay down, with his hand in mine, and let the exhaustion take me. I am asleep before I can even appreciate that the pain is gone. I rest for about half an hour until I hear it.

"Hello! I am just here to check how you are progressing" the nurse says in a sweet whisper.

It is loud enough to wake me up, but quiet enough that you can tell she did not want to disturb the peace.

She drapes the blanket back and begins her check, "Do you feel any pressure?" she asks.

"I don't feel anything."

"Oh! Wow. It's time to set up for delivery, I will page your midwife" she says with a less-than-calm urgency.

And within seconds, Margie my midwife, came into my room running.

For an old lady, she runs fast. She plops a cap on top of her white hair and pushes up her glasses. She immediately starts preparing for delivery without as much as a hello. She put on her robe and gloves and draped me to provide the privacy I asked for. She has memorized my birth plan and has everything perfectly prepared in seconds. She is a wizard, I swear.

Will stands up by my head and holds my hand. His mother stands behind him, and my mom stands on the other side and places her hand in mine. It was time, the baby was crowning.

"You can do this baby," my mom says to me.

All I can think about before it is time to push my daughter out into this world is how loved she will be. In the waiting room, my family and Will's family sit together and pray over our tiny bundle of joy. Our families have come together in the most beautiful way I could have hoped. In a way where both sides wrapped around us in love and support, willing to do anything to help us succeed. We owe so much to them all. I am feeling lucky.

"It is time to start pushing my dear," says Margie.

I cannot feel anything but joy. I go for it.

"Wow! She has a beautiful head of hair, just like mom," Margie continues.

And in only fifteen minutes and three pushes, I am looking at the tiniest, most wonderful, beautiful baby girl on my chest and she is mine.

"I love you, Presley," I say as I kiss her tiny round head that is covered in fuzzy dark hair. Hair that would soon fall out and come back a golden blonde.

When I look into her pure blue eyes, I lose myself in the love that I feel. Like nothing else in the entire universe matters and eight years later, her eyes still do that to me.

She is here. She is healthy. She is perfect.

Will climbs into bed next to me and as I look at him and look at her, I find it hard to believe what I see. I have a family of my own and I can't come up with a reason for why I deserve this. I feel like God has forgiven me, through this blessing and it overwhelms my entire existence.

I knew that I loved this man, but I didn't know how much. My love for him became something stronger, something different, something more, the second I watched him become a father.

My brother Scott is in the waiting room prepared to meet Presley. I know he is impatient, so I am sure he is getting antsy. I made him a promise a while back and now I am ready to honor it. I am ready to witness the moment that doctors swore to us would never come. I am ready to witness the second miracle of the day.

When it is time for visitors, Scott walks in with my dad, unsteady, but here he comes. My dad helps him walk with unsteady steps and guides him over to the couch. He helps Scott as he lowers himself to sit down. My father reaches toward me and grabs Presley from my arms. As he takes her, his hands cover her entire body. He sneaks in a quick squeeze for himself. I see him look at her the same way he looks at me, and the tears greet my eyes. I watch as he slowly, but surely places her into Scott's hands.

"You got her, son?" he asks a bit uncertain.

"I got her," Scott responds.

He says it with shaking hands, but a steady voice. And now tears are running down my cheeks. To see her tiny body in his massive hands may be one of the most precious encounters to see. My entire pregnancy I prayed for this moment and now it is here. She got to meet her uncle.

* * *

This was a room that, while incredible, was also in some respects difficult to accept. This room taught me that I was never going to be brand new. That I just simply had to accept that perfection could never be maintained. I had to change, and I had to love myself, past included. She was too incredible not to. This was one of the best and hardest rooms of all, as motherhood often is. Because as much as I was willing to do the work, now I was on a deadline.

If it is true what they say that your mess is your message, I had to figure out what I wanted mine to be.

Did I want to be the girl I was? The girl who got completely taken over by trauma, tragedy and grief?

Or did I want redemption?

Did I want to pick myself back up after every time I got knocked down? Did I want to get up and heal anyway? Love anyway? Find happiness in any small moment I can find?

Getting pregnant with my daughter answered so many questions for me. I didn't want her mom to be a woman who let her pain take her under. I wanted her to have a mother who could fight. Who could get up, dust herself off and keep walking even if the steps were shaky. That's the kind of woman I wanted her to grow up to be. So, I was going to have to set that example.

Chapter 19: Endless Love

The door is white and enchanting. It is covered in lace and while it is simple, it pulls you in with its warmth and its promise. It is my wedding day. But before I can go in, even though I am dying to, I make Will promise me this one thing. We will go to therapy for at least a year together, that way, when we walk through this door together, we will arrive strong and steady.

There is no such thing as a perfect life or a perfect marriage, but I knew that if we did this one thing first, it could give us a fighting chance. The world begs us to pretend like we can achieve this idealist, perfectionist life and marriage, but what I knew to be true, was that this was a lie and I craved something real.

What I knew was the fewer truths we share, the more disconnected and alone we will feel. I craved a relationship rooted in transparency and trust. I wanted to go through therapy first to tackle the potential problems and hard conversations head-on. I wanted to lay the groundwork for a stronger foundation, for a stable one. I knew it would be messy and beautiful, but what I wanted to know was that it could go the distance. For it to last, we both needed to be very upfront and honest with ourselves and each other with our needs.

The first thing I did was take him into my rooms. I let him see me in ways that only my therapist and my family have. I let him walk through every door and dig around. I let him in on every uncovered secret, every buried mistake, no matter how painful. And then he would do the same.

The process filled me up even more than it challenged me. I was afraid to show the man I loved most who I was underneath the pretty picture. I was afraid to let him know me. I was convinced that he would not love me once he saw all the baggage I was carrying. But I did it anyway. To get the love I wanted, I had to.

I opened the doors, I took him inside, and I showed him all the parts of me that I had been hiding away. When I was done, our therapist gave me a smile and asked him the ultimate question.

"How do you feel about everything she just shared?"

There is a long pause, I can tell that he is trying to take it all in.

"I don't feel any differently. I hate that she went through all of that, but I still look at her the same."

Our therapist looked at me. I was bubbling up in a mess of tears that refused to be held down anymore.

"How do you feel about what he just said?"

"Scared" I say, "that he will look at me differently."

I feel Will take my hand in his. His touch is gentle, but his grip is firm. He is confirming that he is with me in this. And then he looks at me.

"I would never judge you. Everything you went through and everything you did helped you become who you are now, and I love who you are now. I don't care about your past."

He somehow manages to say everything I need to hear.

I doubt my husband Will ever thinks about this conversation because to him it was a "duh" and easy moment. Probably because he is a great human. But to me, it meant everything. It is a conversation I hold onto and remember often. Here I was sharing things that I was convinced would make him change his mind and decide not to marry me anymore. Convinced that all these things made me unworthy of his love, yet here he is, saying he is still with me.

It gave us the most significant foundation we needed, which was trust.

On the day of our wedding, I would rely on this foundation with my heart and soul. This day, while whimsical and enchanting, was incredibly stressful and scary. I would tune into his words and everything we promised each other in the months leading up to this day. It is June 10, 2017. I am twenty-three years old, I am a mother, and I am getting married.

My sister Kendra surprised me with the most beautiful wedding gift. It is a gift only she could give me, and it is something that holds a massive amount of heartfelt goodness. It is more than anyone could ask for or imagine. Every bride needs something blue, that is the tradition. To be honest, I have no clue why, I just knew I was supposed to have something. But, me being me, I did not have one because going against traditions and rules is in my nature.

It is finally time to put on the dress. The dress that I picked out in a photo. The dress that my mom, Presley and I flew to Las Vegas to get. I knew the second I saw it, that it was my dress. It has a fully beaded mermaid bodice and these beautiful wave-like ruffles that come out of the bottom. I love the way it flows like water. The way it sparkles and lights up with every turn. I was dying to get into it.

The last time I was in this dress was when I tried it on in that boutique.

When the three of us stepped into the shop, my dress was the centerpiece of the store. It hugged tightly around a mannequin.

"Oh my word, look at that one," my mother said, pointing at it "That is stunning."

"Yep. There she is."

"That's the one?"

"It is" I assured her.

The woman who was working behind the counter quickly began undressing the mannequin and handed the dress to me.

"This is the only one we have, but we can mail you one in your size," she said as she closed the changing room door.

Then, I came out of that dressing room and stepped onto that lit-up platform covered in mirrors. Presley looked up at me, and the look in her eyes was all I needed.

"This is the one" I said as I admired every detail in the mirror. "This is the one."

We all knew it. I didn't need to try on anything else.

That's why today, on my wedding day, I am dying to put that dress on. To feel that beautiful again. To see my daughter look at me like that one more time.

I grab the sides and step in. The wedding isn't for another couple of hours, but we need to get some bridal photos done before I cry all of this makeup off. As I pulled the dress on, I began squirming it up my body and when I got it to my stomach, I saw Kendra's gift. A navy-blue heart.

The fabric of the heart is old and worn and has stitching just along the edges to attach it to my gown. Without any need for explanation, I know what my sister has done. I recognize this fabric. This heart came from my brother Ryan's shirt. I know that my sister has cut this out and sewn this on for me. I lifted my head up and tilted it back in hopes of stopping the tears. I blink until they go away and then I take a breath.

"I know you are here with me today" I whispered to the heart hoping he could hear me.

And now with his heart on mine, at least in some tangible way, he can be here for his baby sister's wedding.

My wedding day was full of emotions. I have all the good excited ones that I am supposed to have. I have all the sad ones that come with acknowledging an empty spot in the grooms-men's line where my brother should be. But, bigger than my other feelings, I have an overwhelming amount of gratitude that the rest of my family and the new family I am marrying into are here to celebrate with us today.

As my friend Jessica curls my long, dark hair, I play with a fidget cube until my hands begin to cramp. I am aggressively messing with it in hopes of easing my nerves. I don't know why I am so scared, we already have a baby together and this should be easy. But it isn't. It is terrifying. I am going to be the star of the show and that level of spotlight makes my anxiety scream.

"I am so happy for you Ash," Jess says to me as she wraps my hair around the iron.

What is a simple phrase packs a lot of meaning. She is one of my few friends who truly saw how bad my past relationship was because she was there for most of it. She prayed for this moment just as much as I did. All her cries and begging me to leave Cody finally came true.

Now, here I was, about to marry someone so unlike my past, someone who was the epitome of what I craved in my future. Someone who for the very first time, I loved.

There is a knock on the door and then I hear the voice that always calms me.

"Honey, it's mom."

"Come in" I reply.

"Time for your veil" she says as she picks it up off the back of the couch.

The veil is white and trimmed with tiny rhinestones. She begins bobby-pinning it into my hair while she fans her watering eyes. She is doing everything in her power not to cry.

I looked in the mirror at myself and tried to take it all in. In seeing me, I can see so many others.

I see a little bit of all of my family here with me. The tiara on my head that my sister Keena made just for me. My brown eyes, that look just like my mother's. My full lips look just like my dad's. My smile that perfectly mimics the one of his mother's, a late grandmother of mine that I never got to meet. I see this beautiful, embellished dress that grips my body, but I know that a secret blue heart from Ryan is here underneath. In which brings me to the gesture itself, I see my sister Kendra's love and thoughtfulness for me. I see my tattoos that cover my biceps, the ones that say "Miller Strong" as a tribute to my brother Scott and his fight with cancer. It wouldn't just be me walking down this aisle today. They would all be with me.

My mom kisses my cheek.

"You look perfect, I will see you soon" she says with a wink as she exits.

"Knock, knock" my father says as he enters my bridal suite.

I turn to meet his gaze.

"Wow" he says with tear-filled eyes.

"You look beautiful, honey."

"Thanks Dad" I say as I wrap him in my arms.

I step back and grab his arm, I give him an "I got this glance" and we step into the hall.

It's time.

We walk down the stairs and finally come to a stop just outside the building. We wait for the bridal party to walk down the aisle and take their place as we slowly, but surely get closer to the aisle.

I small talk my dad the entire way walking towards the entrance. I don't even know what I am saying, just random, nervous, mumbling. What had Willie signed up for? *A lifetime of listening to nervous rambles, that's what*, I think to myself.

My daughter was just as nervous as me. Walking in front of all these people was a lot for me and I was twenty-three. She was two and I asked her to do the same thing. I somehow pulled a trick from *Big Daddy* and convinced her that these little white polka-dotted glasses would make her invisible. All she had to do was put them on and walk to her dad. She was so much braver than me. It worked like a charm. I needed to thank Adam Sandler for that one.

She took off down the path following my two older nieces in front of her. I was too far back to see, but when I watched the video, it was hard to decide what was sweeter. Our baby girl walking down the aisle, getting to be a part of this moment, or my husband sobbing as he watched her take each step.

As I round the corner, I can finally see him standing there. He is at the end of the aisle and if I could run to him, I would. My eyes instantly well up with tears. I have never really seen Will cry before, yet here he is, letting those tears fall at rapid rates. I watch as he drops his head in disbelief, lifts his glasses to wipe away his tears, and looks at me like no one has ever looked at me before. I have never loved him more.

He chose to love me. *I was worth loving.* And I chose him.

The woman we hired to marry us has begun her speech. She has made it incredibly personal, and I am honored that she knows our story so well. As much as it sounds like a damsel in distress fairy tale, it kind of is one. The feminist in me secretly hates the way this sounds, but the realist in me knew that I could save myself, that I did save myself, but it was okay that I let him help me.

We wrote our own vows, something that was extremely important to us both and to my surprise I was able to say them without a stumble. I fought tears back as I read them off, but with his hand in mine it was easy to feel stable, to let the nerves wash away, to feel safe.

* * *

"Babe, wake up. Babe, what's wrong?" I hear my husband saying a bit loudly for the middle of the night.

His touch startles me, but not as much as the tears running down my face and the uncontrollable shaking of my body. *How was that a dream?* And why would my brain do that to me? It felt so real.

That has never happened to me before. I have never dreamed of a past moment so intensely that I have sobbed in my sleep, that

I have panicked in my sleep. The feelings I had in the dream mimicked perfectly of a memory. The despair, the inability to fight back to make it stop, it was all there. It invited conversations that even after being married for a year, I wasn't ready to have with my husband, conversations I even avoided with my therapist.

My now husband, forever patient and forever kind, pulled me into his arms.

"It's okay babe, you don't have to tell me right now."

One of the many things I loved about him, he wasn't going to push me into anything before I was ready. He knew that in this moment, I didn't need to talk, I just needed to feel loved, to feel protected, to lay in his arms and let the safety of being with him sink in.

There were too many misconceptions in my head from the dream. It felt like too much and I didn't have the courage to work it out just yet.

All I was able to give my thankfully very understanding and worried husband was that I had a nightmare. I had a nightmare about my past and it was something I wasn't ready to unpack yet. It is hard to discuss something you don't fully understand yourself.

The anxiety comes from the anger, the anger at Cody is big, but the anger at myself is all-consuming. Why didn't I fight harder? Why did I just say no and cry through it? Why did I let this happen? I don't know. I know at the time, I didn't believe

I was worth fighting for, I know that for certain. I know that I was engulfed in the fear that if I truly fought back, and he still didn't stop, that I would become a victim. I didn't think I could cope with that risk. My brain really convinced me that to stay safe, I needed to give in. To not rock the boat. My tried-and-true strategy that I carried with me since I was a kid.

And now I am almost thirty, praying with every inch of me that I raise daughters who will fight like hell for themselves. I want them to feel powerful when they are young women. Because all I felt like I was during this nightmare- was an empty, shame-filled shell.

I didn't want my daughters to make the same mistakes that I made. So, I was determined to figure out why I made them, to hopefully prevent them from doing the same. I didn't want them to have to learn the hard way, I just wanted them to have peace. So, I fought through therapy to find it. And then to use what I learned to raise someone different. I wanted to give them a past that would be worth chasing in the future. If they can fall in love with someone who is similar to their father, then I know they'll be in good hands.

Setting this standard for myself and for my daughters would feel like such a win. I want to forever set us up for the best outcome. They deserve the world and more. They deserve the beautiful calm that my husband brings me.

When I look into my daughter's crystal blue eyes, the ones she inherited from her father, all I see is a pool of abundance. That is how this life feels. So abundant with love. With joy. With hurt and hugs. The worst of times have forever taught me how to soak up all the tiny goodness and for that, I am always grateful.

As I go through these rooms, I am facing my biggest fears and tearing through my worst heartaches to heal so I can raise my daughter in peace. So, I can love my husband in peace. That is what I am chasing.

Presley is calm, she is happy, and she is incredibly loved and so am I. It's hard to explain how good it feels to be completely accepting and understanding of ourselves and of others. Of how good it feels to be loved and loved well.

My favorite parts of marriage are not the big romantic gestures or the honeymoon phase, although both of those are lovely. My favorite parts of marriage are simple and ordinary. It's watching my husband take care of our family. It's seeing him across the dinner table with a tiara on his head and clip-on earrings in his ears. It's watching him do anything and everything to make our girls smile. It's the way he looks at me, the safety he makes me feel, the way he still can't resist me or tell me no. The way he is there. He is always there for me. It is the way that we know each other, like the back of our hands, the trust that wraps around you like a hug. It's everything small that he does every single day. That's why I love our marriage.

We feel pressure all the time to be the perfect parent, perfect spouse, perfect human. But the goodness isn't in the grandiosity. The goodness is in the everyday small moments that bring us joy. Having someone to come home to, to eat with, to laugh with, to lean on, to love.

The only thing pressure does is burst, so we took it off. We took things slowly. Once we had our daughter, we knew there was pressure to get married, to stay together, but we didn't want it that way. We wanted to choose each other and with each step of the way, we did.

Day after day, he chose me, and I chose him. I walked into this love with him with careful and certain steps that he was everything I wanted and more. I knew that without a shadow of a doubt, he was the one for me.

I hoped we could set this example for our kids. To show them how to walk steadily. How to make their own choices without being impulsive or giving in to the pressures around them. But instead, to make choices that bring them the most joy. The most peace. The most calm. Without pressure or perfectionism, it is amazing how things can bloom. That's what I wanted for them.

Happiness and peace, in any form that they wish.

I learned that there is no such thing as the perfect parent, wife, or person. I had to force myself to accept that we will indeed leave our kids with some issues. I had to own the fact that I will one thousand percent make many mistakes. And I had to get real with myself, that if I want to raise resilient kids, then they are going to have to struggle. I had to get real with myself on the same thing with my marriage. In order to strengthen it, we would have to overcome adversities. And we did, and we would, and we would grow to become closer than ever. This room would become my forever.

Chapter 20:
Waves of Worry

The door is light pink and covered in wild patterns. It is everchanging and swarmed with flowers. It is blooming. It is ready to be opened. I grab the vine and untie it from the handle. I push it down and on one quick stride, the door swings and I am inside.

Immediately after the wedding, we started trying for another baby. We sincerely hoped that we would time it exactly right. We already had one kid with a birthday a week before Christmas and as magical as that is, it's expensive. We prayed for a summer baby, one that would eventually meet us in June.

Everything went according to plan, everything except for the fact that the baby was breech.

Having a breech baby wasn't exactly in my birth plans. I know I said my first experience with labor was the most physical pain I had ever been in, but that was before I had a doctor on top of me, on all fours, trying to flip a baby into the correct position while it was still in my stomach.

My husband compared it to aliens. You could physically see the baby's body outline through my stomach as the doctor tried to flip her into the correct upside-down position. It nearly broke my pelvis, as the baby was already engaged, ready to go, bottom first. As the doctor pushed the head out of my ribs, she used the other hand to grab the baby's butt and legs and turn her. Moving her head out of my ribs knocked the wind out of me, but once she pushed on the butt, the screams that escaped my mouth were animalistic, it felt like a slow-motion breaking of my bones.

"I'm done" I barely breathed out "I'm done."

I had to give up and accept my fate. I had to schedule a c-section.

Trying to give birth to a breech baby wasn't even an option. We made the appointment for the c-section, June 7th at 7:30 in the morning. In just two weeks' time, I will be meeting my second baby girl, Everly. The thought of being cut in half didn't appeal to me, but getting this baby out sounded nice.

This pregnancy was way less comfortable than my first one. While I was not nearly as sick, I was in far more pain. I am assuming it's because breech babies don't fit in the stomach as comfortably because they aren't supposed to be sitting straight up with their head in your ribs in the first place. It felt like there was not enough room and I couldn't wait to gain full lung capacity back again.

The two weeks passed slowly, and I tried to soak up every second of Presley being an only child. We did all the fun things that she loved that might have to be put on hold for a while until the baby got here. We redid her room and focused on all the exciting things that being a big sister would bring her. Watching her eyes light up every time the word sister was mentioned would be the most precious memory up until I saw her face when she finally became one.

As I drove Presley to my in-law's house, we talked about what she could expect when she came to visit us in the hospital. I wanted to prepare her without scaring her too much. I wanted her to feel prepared and comfortable when she came in. I warned her that I was getting surgery, and that mommy would be in pain, and she would not be able to move around much. And I told her that her sister would be tiny and delicate, but she could hold her as long as she was careful. I prepared her for the reality I was prepared for, for the one I hoped we would get.

When we arrived, I felt a sense of sadness wash over me, over us both. We were never apart, I barely worked, just one day sometimes two a week at the salon and we had only ever been apart for two overnights and not consecutively. And one of those nights was the wedding. I had a tough time leaving Presley anywhere.

My PTSD which I had been diagnosed with in therapy reared its head in these moments. Even though my in-laws were the most incredible people, it didn't help. I could be leaving her with Jesus Himself, and I would still feel sick with fear. I held onto her so tight, like my life depended on her being okay. It was an issue that I would continue to work out. It was my task to learn how to feel safe.

At three, her blonde hair just brushed the tips of her shoulders and her sapphire eyes looked right at me. I picked her up for a hug and relished the way it felt when her tiny arms squeezed around my neck. Even though I couldn't breathe, I loved these moments. I put her down, knowing I wouldn't be picking her up for a while and kissed her cheek before I left.

My husband drove the two of us, and by the time we got to the hospital, there was no time to process. Will parked our car and as soon as we walked in, they immediately took me back and began preparing me for surgery. This included many unfun things, but my least favorite was how they strapped my legs and hands down to the table. My arms laid out in a "T" shape while I was bound at the wrists and my legs straight strapped down by my ankles.

"It's for your safety. Since you won't be able to feel anything, we can't risk you reaching around or anything," the nurse assured me as she saw the fear in my eyes.

They started administering some medication to help me relax, it was nearly impossible to feel calm. I was overflowing with anxiety. I felt claustrophobic from the straps and the thought of being awake for surgery seriously creeps me out. Plus, I was having a baby today. It's not a calm thing.

I looked to my left and saw that everything was set up for the baby. Then, I turned my head and looked to my right and saw the medicine cabinet that was covered by a glass door. I was quick to realize I could see a reflection in the glass, I instantly looked to the ceiling and made sure not to look that way again. I did not want to watch what was about to happen to me.

I couldn't imagine what they were about to do to me without feeling extremely sick and anxious. I watched as the nurses worked together to hang a blue sheet up right below my chest. This would allow the surgery to occur in the privacy of the doctor's eyes while my husband and I could hide behind it. I couldn't see anything other than the ceiling and my anesthesiologist, who sat by my head and tried to keep me comfortable. He was the only one who communicated with me throughout the process because everyone's focus would be on the baby. Eventually, they brought my husband in. I had never seen him in a hospital gown and cap before, so it was quite a comedic relief for me.

The uncomfortable nervousness started to flood me. The surgery started immediately after he sat down and put his hand on my shoulder. The second I heard the tool buzz, the smell of burning flesh filled the room, and I started awkwardly small talking my husband. I needed a distraction. I needed to pretend like this wasn't happening to me to stay calm.

The drilling sounds from the surgeon's tools pierced my ears and filled my head. I was forcing myself to think about anything other than being opened up on this table. I used to be so good at this, at taking myself out of the moments that were hard for me, and imagining I was somewhere else. But years of therapy have made me in sync with the truth, so much so, that I cannot escape it anymore, no matter how hard I try. Once you gain awareness, you can't go back to pretending.

I knew my only option was to accept reality and tough it out. All that mattered to me right now, was my baby, so I focused on that. Within what felt like seconds, I felt the doctor's hands.

"You are going to feel a lot of pressure" my midwife warned me.

And I did. I felt a huge weight, a jerk, a tug, and then I heard, "We have a baby" from my midwife's sweet and subtle voice.

The nurse pulled down a tiny part of the curtain to reveal a beautiful, but very blue baby face to me, "Here she is mama," and then she was gone.

I was expecting her to be brought around to me. I had seen the adorable pictures of the baby being held by the mother's face post-c-section. I was waiting for that moment. I wanted a picture just like that.

I expected to hear crying, to have her wrapped up and brought around to me, but she never came. They gave me a quick peak, and she was gone. All I could hear was panicked nurses, a suctioning sound, and so much fluid. *Why wasn't she crying?*

"Why isn't she crying?" I begged my anesthesiologist, followed with "What is going on? Is she okay?" not really waiting for an answer.

"Looks like they are trying to suck fluid out of her lungs, I am sure she will be fine," he tried to comfort me.

A nurse came around for my husband. "We need you back here with the baby. Would you like to meet your daughter?" she asked him.

"Yeah, of course," he responded.

"Just make sure you shield your eyes as we walk around the surgical table and I'll guide you to your baby" she said, noticing he was a bit squeamish about the entire process.

The nurse took his arm and began to walk him over to her.

I couldn't see anything due to being strapped down. I felt so alone, so helpless, so left out. Time was moving so slowly, and it took forever for them to finish putting me back together and stitching me up. I was begging to see my baby, to see what was wrong with her and no one was telling me anything. I never thought I would feel this scared again, but this fear, this worry of my child, was worse than anything I had ever feared before.

I was in a full-blown panic by the time my stitches were done. As they continued to work on Everly, they moved me into a different room, which only made me worry more. I did not understand why I had to be in post-op, I didn't understand why I couldn't stay with my husband and our baby, and I didn't understand why no one was telling me anything.

My mind wandered to the worst-case scenario, as it often does, and I cried as I waited for someone, anyone, to tell me anything.

The door began to open slowly, and I held my breath. I watched as my husband walked in and I tried to read his face for clues, but then a nurse came in right after him holding our baby. She saw the tears streaming down my face and smiled, "Look, you can hold her for a second. Let's get a picture, but then we have to rush her to the NICU. She has a ton of fluid in her lungs, and we need to help her with her breathing" she said to me as she placed my tiny daughter in my arms.

Her skin so tan, her head so perfectly round, her eyes so blue and her dark hair framed her face much like mine did. It physically hurt so much to hand her back, I wanted to keep her in my arms forever. I was begging for time, but I got two seconds and a photo, as I was promised before they rushed my baby away from me again. It felt like they took her out of me and took her from me. Everything about it went against my natural instincts.

I kissed her tiny hands and handed her back to the nurse. She then took our daughter to the NICU, and my husband followed. "Stay with her," I told him as I was left in the room, alone with nothing, but my worries again.

"It will take about an hour and then we will bring you down to your baby" the nurse reassured me. Luckily, I wasn't waiting in post-op too long before they came to get me and moved me into my new room. This experience was so far from my first that I felt overwhelmed and was struggling to process it all.

A nurse eventually came and wheeled me down from the seventh floor, where I would be staying, to the sixth floor, where my baby would be. It felt so far away. I wasn't prepared for what I would see. I wasn't anticipating the first time I would truly hold my daughter that she would have an IV in her head, monitors strapped to her chest, a feeding tube that streamed from her mouth and was taped to her chin, or the c-pap machine that covered her tiny nose to help her breathe. I couldn't even tell what she looked like with all the equipment covering her up.

I tried to keep my gratitude, as she was one of the healthiest babies in the NICU. But, in so many ways I felt grief. What was supposed to be a perfect and wonderful day, was so lonely, so terrifying, and I felt so helpless. While the miracle of her being here meant everything to me. Seeing her like this overwhelmed me with fears that I felt I could never face. Life is so fragile and when you become a mother, that fragility is terrorizing. It's like having your actual heart walking around outside of your body.

I know now to appreciate the nurses that I felt ignored me. They were very one-track-minded on taking care of my baby and for that, I am so grateful. But at the time, I was so freaked out and so alone. I had just had massive surgery, something was wrong with my baby, and I didn't have a clue what the heck was going on. It was terrifying. I was trying to stay calm, but that's not always my strong suit. I was losing my grip. I was sick with worry. It was taking over me.

Little did I know that motherhood would often feel like this. That the worrying would be like the waves, it would come and go, just like everything else. The moment I had her in my arms, the tears just started pouring. That overwhelming love takes over your entire existence. Here she was, such a gift. I was going to be able to give my daughters the gift of a sister, one I was lucky enough to get twice.

On the morning of June 8th, Presley arrived at the hospital to meet her new baby sister. There was no way to prepare her for the scene. She was three and a half years old, and the hospital felt like a scary place. She was so brave.

She walked in with my mother and father-in-law and immediately crawled into my hospital bed with me. She was so gentle and so careful. She was almost scared to touch me, but I quickly pulled her little blonde self into a hug, and she gave in to my arms.

She was overwhelmed, I could feel it. I held her as they pushed me down to the NICU and I tried to prepare her for what she would see. I wanted to warn her of the things that were attached to Everly, so it wasn't a scary shock or surprise.

As soon as we went in, the nurse grabbed Everly and placed her on my chest. I grabbed the cords and tubes that were attached to her and attempted to move them out of the way so Presley could get up close next to her. She laid her tiny head down on my shoulder and wrapped her little arms around us both. The look in her eyes, as she stared into Evie's, may go down as my favorite memory.

I pray that they have the love and the strong bonds that I have with my siblings. I pray that they never have to go through the hardships that brought me and my siblings close, like how we relied so much on each other just to get through it all, but I prayed that they would have that closeness, that love, that bond, just because they could. Not because they had to. And I prayed that I could do a good enough job as a mom, that someday, when they were all grown up, they would both still come back to me for hugs like this. Our kids don't owe us anything. I chose to bring them into this world, and I could only pray that they would always want to stay in mine.

When I look at Everly now, I see so much of what she showed when she came into this world. Strength. She is an old soul, an empath through and through, more in touch with her emotions at five than many adults I know. She is wild at home where she feels the safest. She knows how to be silly, how to do the perfect villainous laugh, how to entertain. But she is not a trick pony, and she won't let just anyone see her this way. She makes you earn it. She has to trust you and she knows she's worth the wait.

Presley has modeled so much of this to her. She has loved her for exactly who she is, while constantly hyping her up. That's what Presley does, she is so unassuming, she has no clue how fantastic she truly is. She has more confidence and courage at eight than I ever did. She made me a mom, but I can only pray that I will teach her as much as she has taught me. And I am forever grateful for all that she will teach Everly.

I would continue to go to therapy and fight to become the mother that they deserved. I would give it my all to become the woman I wanted to be. And I was getting close.

Chapter 21:
Finding My Purpose

My girls have shown me that the door to motherhood is hard and messy. It's white and it's covered in tiny Cheeto stains from their sticky little fingers. And when I open it and step inside, I am swarmed with hugs instantly. It's the warmest and most beautiful experience. It is full of color and light. I walk in shielded, praying to not let the darkness inside of me seep into it. Is this how we all feel? Is this what we all do? Do we all keep our pain, our trauma, and our guilt inside?

I know I do. I try to hide it from my kids so they can stay innocent and pure. I try to hide it from my husband. I try to save it for myself. I try to protect them from my hurt, I try to give them more.

Regardless of how we grow up, we always want our kids to have something better than we know. It's in our nature. We don't want them to hurt like we do. To have issues like we do. But we must accept that they will.

Having kids is hard and it's easy and plentiful at the same time. It is abundant in joy and threaded by a mother who is simply trying to keep it together.

The hardest part about parenting is not the money, the moments when they're being crazy or acting out. The hardest part about parenting is all the past struggles that it triggers and brings up.

It's having the strength to admit when we don't do the right thing. It is owning those moments when we mess up and then having even more strength to apologize and try to fix it.

It's the guilt we feel because of it. The guilt we feel when we don't react our best. The guilt when we can't make the school event or when we can't stay home when they are sick. When we can't be perfect because we're not. That's when the doubt starts to trickle in. How could we ever be enough?

When we mess up, when we get triggered, and we react in a way that we wish we didn't. When we pass down our issues. When we see that our daughter has the anxiety that we do and then we beat ourselves up for not being better, for not being "perfect."

While therapy has saved my life and made me an entirely better person. This is the area that I still struggle with the most.

I can deal with the nightmares that PTSD brings me from my past. They suck, but I can do it. But when I feel like I am not perfect for my kids, that's the real gut punch that's hard to take. That's the hardest piece for me to accept.

What I have come to understand is that children do not need a perfect parent. They are incredibly forgiving. Every time I mess up, overreact, and let my issues get the best of me, I apologize. It happens often. I own up, I take responsibility, and I apologize to my kids. They are human, just like me, and I try to teach grace over perfection.

I ask for forgiveness, but I never demand it. And I hope more than anything, they learn that it is okay to make mistakes. I don't want them chasing perfection as I do. I don't want them to carry shame for things that they can't control like I did and sometimes still do. I want them to be forgiving to themselves, I want them to get comfortable owning their mistakes and seeing that a change in behavior when you mess up is all that is required.

The goal in life is to learn, not to wallow.

If I don't want them to have the self-deprecating perfectionist mindset that I do, then I need to get comfortable with not being perfect. I need to model to them that being human is okay. I want to raise problem solvers, not perfectionists.

Some of my best qualities I got from my parents come from how they handled themselves when things went wrong.

What my mom sees as her biggest mistakes taught me how to be strong. It showed me what it means to be a woman who can do things all on her own. It taught me how to ask for help when things get too heavy, how to apologize when you screw up and how to bounce back every time life kicks you down. What she saw as her failure, I see as her redemption story. One that would also become mine. One that would bring us closer than ever before. When my mom apologizes to me for the past, because she still does, I just want her to know that all I have for her in my heart is love. I forgave her so long ago. I forgave her when I forgave myself for doing the same thing. I hope she knows how strong she is. I hope she knows how much I love her.

When my dad was young, he lost his mother and his dream. He knows what it feels like to reinvent himself. What he doesn't know was how much it all taught me. He made new dreams, and he made his own come true. He taught me how to fight for my own and how to never give up. How to chase every goal and how to hit the ground running. He showed me that it is possible to keep someone's memory alive even when they're gone. I never met his mom, my grandma, but I've always felt like I know her. He taught me I could do the same for my kids with Ryan.

They taught me that I can use my struggles to help others. To teach my own children. To become the person, I am meant to be.

For me that started with understanding that an apology, without change, is more manipulative than it is kind. An apology should guarantee that in the future, the same mistakes will be avoided as much as possible. Because without the change, "I'm sorry" truly doesn't mean anything. Feeling bad is not enough for forgiveness. Change, is. I want to model this to my kids, so that in the future, they can avoid some of the roads I had to take to learn this. I don't want them to have to go through all these rooms, to get here.

* * *

My last door in therapy would ideally lead me to who I was. We had gone through every tough and beautiful room, and we could clearly see how I ended up where I did. It was no coincidence that once I got the help I needed, my doors started changing and taking me in a new direction. A better one. One's that led to love, forgiveness, peace, and motherhood.

So, as I stand outside this door, I try to take it all in. It's cloudy and incomplete. It floats in the air without hinges or gravity to keep it down. It is free. I can make out the door handle, it looks gold and antique, but the edges of the door are missing, it's completely fogged out. I don't know how to open it. I don't know how to greet the woman inside. As I dug through the rooms of my past, I found so many things that I am not. Under the mess and under the hurt, there were tiny flecks of me, but nothing that was whole. I was left with so many questions. Who is the woman that remains? How do we find her?

My therapist and I explored some of these questions and I began to think of the people I looked up to. I thought about the type of person that I would want to be. I kept that image in my head and when I opened the door, I saw my high-school cheerleading coach. She stood much shorter than me, even in her six-inch-tall heels that she always wore. Her shoulder-length blonde hair framed a confident face and her outfits always looked perfectly put together and pretty expensive. She meant business. The epitome of tough love. I wasn't surprised to see her here.

It comes as no surprise that this cheer coach of mine was one of the absolute best mentors and role models I had in my life. I was lucky enough to have her as a teacher as well. She taught my favorite subject, English, and up until her class I didn't enjoy school much. She was the only teacher I ever had who I felt like knew me. I wasn't another body in the room to teach. I was a person and one worth knowing. I felt seen and loved for the first time at school and it made me want to work even harder for her.

She didn't know what it meant for me at the time. No one at the school really knew me, not even my teammates. The only people at that school that I let get to know me was my best friend Kenzi and my coach.

We would be crammed into tiny, horrific smelling classrooms, surrounded by our peers and I would somehow still feel like I was all alone. Like no one could really see me, because what they saw versus who I was, was insanely different. They saw a stuck-up cheerleader, but what they didn't know was that my brother had cancer, I was searching for ways to cope with the abuse of my stepfather, and I had no emotional room to pretend like I was happy to be here. What they didn't know was that cheerleading and my coach were the only reasons I finished high school.

What they did not know was that I was dying to be honest, to open up, but I had learned the risk of honesty, and it was not worth it. The one time I opened up to another teacher I wrote a letter. We were tasked with an assignment after reading *The Great Gatsby* to write a letter about anger. It was handwritten and man did it come flying out onto the paper. It was due at the end of the hour, but that's not why I was rushing. I was rushing because I had never told anyone this before and it was dying to come out.

I was screaming through handwritten words. I was mad at everyone, even though few people knew what had happened or about everything my stepfather did. I was enraged. I was unrelenting that so much was stolen from me so young.

I will never feel safe again because of YOU.

I finished the letter. All capital letters and underlined. I threw it in the turn-in basket and let my teacher read my screw you letter to the world.

Sincerely, me.

The next day, that same teacher would pull me into the hall to talk. *Oh crap.* I figured I was in trouble for letting my crazy shine.

"So" she started calmly with her voice so low I could barely hear her "I read your letter and I wanted you to know that I had to turn it in. The counselor is waiting in his office for you if you would like to head down there."

Sounded a lot less like a question, because, no I don't want to, but obviously, she was insinuating that I had to.

My head was shaking nonstop, "No, no, no you can't turn it in. I gave that to you for you to read. You promised you were the only one that was going to read it" I said.

I was pissed off and feeling betrayed.

"Ashleigh, I am a mandated reporter. I have to turn that in. I could lose my job. I'm so sor-"

"You're not sorry!" I snapped "You need to fix this. They

could take me from my mom! How could you do this?" I yelled with shaking hands and the utter despair of feeling the world rip out from under me.

"How could you?" I asked as I looked at her through my tear-filled eyes.

I shook my head in disbelief and went to the counselors. Only to pass Cody on the way down. He would ask for years about this day, but I would never tell him.

"I don't believe you, but I can't help you if you aren't honest with me," my counselor said after I was forced to explain my letter.

"Welp, that's the truth. I'm a writer, I made it all up. It's not true. Just a story."

"Maybe, but I think it's your story," he said as he dialed a report line.

"Now, Ashleigh read the letter to her and tell them what you told me."

I did as I was told. Then, I told them I made it all up. And even though they knew I was lying, they couldn't do anything about it.

We hadn't lived with my stepfather for years, it wasn't worth reporting. I knew that there was no way they could help me, even though they wanted to. The damage was done and me and my mom were going to get through this. I didn't need people to save me. I needed someone to hear me. To listen. But I wasn't allowed to talk about it with anyone because if I did, they got so lost in trying to "fix it" when all I needed was to be heard. To be understood. That's what ate me up. Trying to make sense of the insensible as a kid.

I left his office and went straight to my coach. She let me cry and hide in her office the rest of the day. People like my coach are impossible to forget because they help shape you into the person, they know you can become. They see past all your teenage crap and know that somewhere in that marble, with enough chiseling, someone amazing lies inside. They take you in as you are and love you for it. Then, they put in the work to help guide you to the person you can become.

* * *

I knew now, why this door led me here. I was supposed to follow in her footsteps and become a teacher myself. I would pick up my own chisel along the way and I too would find the beauty in the kids who suffered under so much marble.

I was happy with my husband and overjoyed with my daughter, but I wasn't even close to being happy with the work I was doing and now I knew why. I drove to my dad's work, he is often the person I reach to when I need wisdom and guidance in regard to any life decision. Mostly because he is extremely lev-elheaded and can see things clearly regardless of all the clouds.

I walked into his car dealership and b-lined it straight into his office, tears in my eyes were already building. I sat in the chair with Presley on my lap and immediately started dumping.

"I'm not happy, dad. I always wanted to graduate college and I dropped out. I don't really like doing hair, it is a great job, but it's not for me. I want a job that I love. I want to make a difference and I want a job that means something to me. I want to be a teacher."

To which he calmly replied, "You are not failing, I can help you, what do you need?"

And it was that easy. He agreed that I needed to go back to school, and he promised to help me through it.

"And by the way Ash, you'll make a great teacher" he said to me.

I could tell he was proud of me and I assumed that he was even relieved. When Ryan died, my dad's girlfriend, who was now my stepmom was quite sure I was going to be next. That's why we fought so much, she was worried about me. She loved me. She knew that after his death, all I did was dance around danger and trouble. And even though she helped me get into the beauty industry, she was so excited for me now.

I worried that she would be upset, but really, we were both just grateful for the times it brought us together and the closeness it helped us feel. While I wasn't in cosmetology for the long run, it was an effective way to keep me busy as I got my life together. No matter what I was doing, they were both just happy to see me care about my life again, regardless of how I did it.

I enrolled in college the next day and I threw myself into it. Once I have a dream, I am laser-focused and ready.

The once not smart enough girl had become a straight-A student. Turns out it was not about what I could do, but what I was willing to do and that is a life lesson in itself. What I thought I could do and what I was actually capable of were two vastly different things. The only thing in my way, was myself.

Without pause, I would graduate college and embark on my new life as a teacher. I often find myself looking for kids who are like me. The ones who seem fine on the surface, but deep down, they are dying to be seen. I tend to search for those alternative kids, the hard to loves, the outcasts, the troublemakers. Those kids need someone, and I try to be to them, what my cheer coach Tracy was to me. I try to be a safe space for them to feel accepted and loved. While in turn, not enabling them to continue on the path they are on.

There is something to be said about loving someone enough to really get on their nerves. That is how lives are changed. When you love a kid enough to call them out on their actions, to teach them, and to love and not judge them every step of the way. In my opinion, every kid needs this, even the "easy" ones if that is a thing. Adults need it too.

As an adult, I often search for mentors who will treat me with the same sort of tough-love approach. I am not one to crave a coddle. I want to grow and to get better all the time. I just need to know that I am loved before I can do it.

In my life, I've been fortunate enough to have what I consider the best of mentors. From my family to my coach, to my therapist. They all helped me find my way. We aren't made to get through this life alone. People are not designed that way.

The goal is to be willing to look inside yourself and to truly own all that you are. Give yourself grace when needed and when you need to do better, try your best to improve. It is a never-ending process, and I am the queen of failing forward. Most of my circle will refer to me as being "too hard on myself," but just like my father, I constantly crave to be better, to do more, to never stop improving. I am so much like him in that way.

It can come with complexities, like never feeling like anything is good enough. I have unfortunately made many feel that way, mostly myself. It has never been about anyone else, though. I love people who come into my life for exactly who they are. But when it comes to myself, I always see the gaps, the unmet goals, the room for improvement, the room for growth, and the never-ending project. As harsh as it sounds and as hard as it has been, I have grown to like this about me.

I just have to stop and remind myself that I am good enough, even without those things, but that doesn't mean that I should stop where I am at. That doesn't mean I should stop chasing improvement, as long as I honor the worthiness of who I am now. Of whom I always was, even at my worst. I even try to admire it.

I am not aiming to become a millionaire, I am a teacher in America for crying out loud, but I am aiming for greatness in regard to the person I become. Whether I am rich, poor, or in between, I just want to be a person who makes others feel loved, inspired, and valued. I just want to help guide people through their tough rooms and to help them find a path to peace.

To serendipity, because the greatest parts of my job, the ones that make it incredibly worth it, are the things that kids say at the end of the year. It's the notes they write, the cards they make and the pictures they draw. I save every single one. It's those tear-filled hugs goodbye as they leave for bigger things. It's the "you changed my life for the better" words. It is all of those small wins, that make me feel like I am making a difference.

People often say, "Choose a job you love, and you will never have to work a day in your life." That is what teaching became for me. And truthfully, that is all I ever wanted. This is my dream, and now, I am living it.

Chapter 22:
I Stayed with Me

When I get up in the morning, I can't believe this is real. I can't believe that behind that foggy door, all of this was waiting for me.

The gigantic white comforter buries my body, and it is so dang comfortable that it is nearly impossible to get up and out of this bed. I finally turn off my alarms, yes multiple alarms. I set about four to ensure that I wake up in the morning. My poor husband, who doesn't need to get up for another three hours, gets woken up by my alarms every morning without a complaint.

My husband. I love saying those words. I love calling him that. I don't know if it's because I lived my whole young life thinking I would never get married and have kids, or if it's just because I simply feel so insanely blessed every time I look at him.

My past self never expected to end up with someone like this. I often can't believe this is all real. That the life I wished for is here. My husband is asleep next to me. Our wonderful and wild daughters are upstairs, still sleeping soundly, most likely cuddling like they always are, it is the cutest thing you've ever seen, and I am sitting in our bed typing this chapter. But in a few minutes, I'll be sitting on my bathroom sink like a perched-up bird doing my makeup, getting ready for my dream job as a teacher.

More things that I love to say, I am a mom. I am a teacher.

When I think back on all my rooms, I find reasons to be grateful for each and every one of them.

I am thankful that my toxic relationship forced me to face my past. If I had never gone through that, I would have never gone to therapy and got the help I truly needed. I am thankful for the experience. While it broke me down in so many ways, it also was a key component in my reasoning for building myself up again.

While losing my brother Ryan was one of the worst things that ever happened to me, it taught me so many important things. And for that I am grateful. I learned that a life without purpose is not much of a life at all. I learned that life is way too short, and you'd better spend it doing something you love. So, I am. I am spending my days as a wife, a mother, a teacher, and an author who is writing this book. All of these things that I love with every ounce of my being because they give me purpose and light me up. And I hope with all my heart that I can make him proud of me, that Ryan can see that I made it out of the dirt.

I am thankful for my childhood. While it was joyous and wonderful, I am thankful for the hard parts too. The ones that taught me how to survive and how to fight like hell when life gets tough.

I am thankful for how close it brought me to my mother and to my siblings. I am grateful that she gifted me with two extra brothers. I hope they both know how loved they are. They came to us at a challenging time, but I am so glad they are in our family now. I owe a lot to my mother, for she taught me how to be one hell of a mom.

I am grateful to have a father who is the epitome of determination. He has shown me how to be humble and how to listen. How to work hard, how to chase my dreams and how to have fun while doing it. How important it is to be more than just pretty and to be something more. How to invest in myself and how to believe I'm worth it.

I learned to accept that the revolving door of my brother's illness was plentiful in blessings as much as it is pain. While his undeniable suffering is beyond heartbreaking and unfair, I find solace and peace in the way that he always beats the odds that are against him. Even now, as we are staring down a tough road ahead as we wait to see if he is eligible for a lung transplant. As we debate in our minds what we want to hear from these doctors. We know the odds aren't great either way. Whether he gets one or not, we don't know what to hope for. What we do know, is that the odds have never been in his favor- yet here he remains. I can only pray that he continues his pattern one last time. I can only pray for him to make it through this. Deep in my core, I believe that he will.

I learned that the best way to spend time is to be with the people you love, to be with family. I learned that it truly is now or possibly never. You never know when it is your time. I learned to soak it all up. I learned that you could do this even from an entire state away. While my sister Keena lives in Texas and I in Colorado, I am closer to her now than ever. She makes sure of it with her daily calls that I always look forward to. I look up to her in every way. She is in many ways, my hero.

I learned that even though Kendra kind of wanted me to get kidnapped as a kid, that we could still become best friends. That she was deep down rooting for me even if she didn't want to admit it back then. She would go on to give me a home and support when I needed it most.

I learned that my family was everything to me. I learned that no amount of time would ever be enough. I learned that being the last of five was equally hard and wonderful. That while I had to grieve as each of my siblings left me behind as they grew up and left home, I was always going to be with them in one sense or another. They would carry me with them, and I would forever do the same. I was not left behind as I so often felt, they were waiting for me on the other side. The five would be forever, whether we had time or not.

I wish I didn't waste so much of my time being bitter. I wish I had gotten the help that I needed sooner. I wish I would have never carried around shame for what happened to me. I wish I would have known that I deserved more, that I was worthy of love. I wish I wouldn't have wasted a moment. But now that I know these things, I won't. I will keep doing the work to heal, to grow. I will invest in myself because I know that my family and I deserve it. Because wishing on the past won't help me, but these changes have, and they will continue to.

We cannot change our past mistakes, our issues, or our trauma. All we can do is accept that it happened just the way that it did. We can do the work to understand why it happened. We can lean into healing, into self-love, until we can finally forgive ourselves, to forgive others if we wish. We can own up to our parts in it, learn from it, heal from it, and use it to help others.

It is our hardships that make us who we are. And if I really mean that, and I do, I cannot regret that it happened because I love the person I became. If there was any simple advice, I would remind myself and those around me to love themselves like they love others.

You too, deserve the grace you give. You are born worthy. No one can take that away from you.

One thing that every room taught me, was to hold on and what to hold on to. And just as important as holding on, I also learned how to let go. I had to put down all the emotional baggage I had been toting around that was never mine to carry in the first place. Everything that happened to me, whether awful or amazing, completely reshaped my entire belief system. What I thought was breaking me, was shaping me into the woman that I would become.

There were so many moments when I thought I wouldn't make it out, that I truly felt like I couldn't get through it. Like, I wasn't sure if I even wanted to. But, if I would have given up, like I almost did, I would have never gotten here. I wouldn't be back in this bed next to my husband, with our sweet daughters jumping all over us. I wouldn't be here at all. And that is something I can't even imagine missing out on. If I had given in, if I had let the grief drown me, I never would have had my new beginning.

If there was one message, I could tell all kids, one that I needed to hear growing up, it's that it is all worth it. It's worth the suffering to get to the other side. But, if you give up before you get there, you'll never know. You deserve more than to end your story before the good parts. Trust me, they are coming.

When I think back on those words, "I will go to therapy. I don't know what's wrong with me. I can change. I must change. I know it is all my fault. Please stay with me," I can say that I did. I kept my promise to myself.

I can say that I did go to therapy, and it saved my life.

I can say that I found out that there were some "things" wrong with me, but I did the work to get through them.

I can say that I did change for the better and I will never stop. I will always seek to grow and understand more.

I can say that I know some of it was my fault, not all of it, but I am proud to own my part.

And most importantly, I can say that I kept my biggest promise of all.

I stayed with me, and it was so damn worth it.

Acknowledgments

To my editor, Tori Thacher thank you for pouring your heart and soul into my book. You took my story and helped me create something beautiful and wonderful to read.

To my designer, Jason Arias thank you for turning my story into a real-life book. I cannot believe how beautiful it is. Seeing you bring it to life has been a dream come true.

To my mother, for allowing me the space to share our truths with the world in hopes of helping others. You are so brave and incredible mom, I hope this memoir reminds you of that.

To my father, who reminded me that this book was the most important investment I could make. Thank you for believing in me and for helping me get here.

To my brother Ryan, may these words keep you alive and with us in some way. We miss you greatly, this one is for you.

To my sister Keena, may these words bring you peace. I hope that you see how important you are to our family. How important you are to me. You are my hero.

To my sister Kendra, for giving me so much more than a home, but a safe space to grow and find myself. You saved me in so many ways.

To my brother Scott, for your constant love and protection. For being there for me every step of the way, even in your toughest moments.

To Teresa, for showing me that step-parents can love you with their entire hearts. It was not something I knew to be true.

To Robin and Ken, for loving me as your own and for being there for our family every step of the way.

To Kenzi, for being my best friend, my rock, my light. You knew this day would come and you stuck with me until I made it.

To Leah, for being my best friend through all of the dark. Nothing makes me happier than seeing us both make it to the light- just as we promised each other we would when we were kids.

To Pamela Jean, for being the bonus sister I never knew I needed. Your belief in me has meant the world to me through this process.

To Tracy, for accepting me as the crazy teenager I was and for encouraging me to one day become the woman I am. The tough love you gave me forever shaped me into a better woman, mom, teacher and friend.

To Tycee, for the years of therapy that it took to heal. I never thought this level of truth and peace was possible. Your guidance and support truly did save my life.

To my students, I hope you all believe in yourselves the way that I always have.

To Will, for showing me that love truly is patient and kind. For showing me that I had never truly been in love before, not until I met you. For setting the most beautiful example of what a husband can be for our daughters. For loving me for who I am and for who I am becoming, without condition. You are my forever love.

To Presley Grace, the day you were born forever changed my life for the better. You not only made me a mom, but you gave me a purpose, a reason to fight for more. You forever challenge me to chase every dream, to constantly work on myself, and to strive to be a woman you can one day look up to. To be more like you! You are an incredible little girl and I cannot wait to see the woman you become.

To Everly Rae, for bringing the beautiful wild to our family. Your level of empathy is something all people should strive to have. You have shown me that motherhood does not have to be perfect, but it needs to be tender. You have reminded me to approach things with an open heart and an open mind. I cannot wait to see who you grow up to be, you will help so many.

To my readers, Thank you beyond words for reading my story. I hope at the very minimum that my memoir can help you in some way. I hope it encourages you to own your story and all of the rooms inside of it. I hope you find the lessons in those rooms that haunt you and I hope you find healing. Let my memoir be the reminder you need that you are worthy of love and good things, regardless of your history. This story is for you.

-Ashleigh Stevens